TIPS
FOR
TOPS

by Dr. George Rosenkranz

Published by
Devyn Press, Inc.
Louisville, Kentucky

Printed in the United States of America.

Devyn Press, Inc.
151 Thierman Lane
Louisville, KY 40207

ISBN 0-910791-24-4

Contents

Section C - Declarer-Play

Dedication

To The Five Stars of My Family

Edith, Bobby, Jerry, Ricky and Heather,
who have been the source of inspiration for this book.

With all my love

Acknowledgments

I would like to express my thanks to the many people who helped in the preparation of this book:

The American Contract Bridge League for its permission to use articles originally published in the *Bulletin*.

Dick Frey and Eddie Wold for considerable editorial help, constructive discussion and continuous encouragement.

Phillip Alder for his invaluable contribution in editing the manuscript and putting it into final form.

Beatriz Coarasa and Lyn Balfour for technical assistance.

And most of all my tribute goes to the late Johnny Gerber who put me on the right path to winning.

Foreword

Bridge is a game of infinite variety. Using only fifteen words, you have to describe billions of hands. The only way you have to show specific features of the hand during the play is the order in which you follow suit or discard. There are many areas which even practiced partnerships have not discussed. Small wonder, then, that the average player is sometimes at a loss in fairly commonplace situations.

In part, we bridge writers are to blame for that. Economic necessity forces us to pen books that will have a reasonable sale — major publishers are not prepared to consider works with limited appeal. Therefore, much of our *oeuvre* is aimed at beginners or the novice player — those are the categories that encompass the bulk of the bridge *aficionados*.

How fortunate for the average duplicate buff that there are some writers like our good friend George Rosenkranz. He has played with and against all of the world's great players, and he is in a position where he can make the knowledge he has gained available to those who are eager to improve their game. Some of his writing has been devoted to promoting his Romex system, features of which are part of the repertoire of experts everywhere. But he has spent much time writing articles for the A.C.B.L. *Bulletin*, and many of those he has collected and expanded into books that have been well received by his peers.

Now it is our pleasure to introduce his new book. You might not agree with all Dr. Rosenkranz suggests — that is your prerogative. You might decide that all or nothing in this book is suitable for you. Be that as it may — just reading this thought-provoking volume is certain to give you a new, and better, outlook on the game we love.

It is like receiving free lessons from one of the world's leading players and theoreticians.

— Tannah Hirsch

Introduction

Multiplication is vexation,
Division is as bad;
The Rule of three doth puzzle me,
And Practice drives me mad.

Anon. (Elizabethan MS dated 1570)

Karl Marx wrote an essay in 1859 entitled *A Critique of Political Economy* in which he stated: "Mankind always sets itself only such problems as it can solve; since, looking at the matter more closely, it will always be found that the task itself arises only when the material conditions for its solution already exist or are at least in the process of formation."

Bridge is such a fascinating game because it continues to supply problems for which the solutions either have not been discovered or are not guaranteed to work (the luck element). Throughout this book are a selection of suggested treatments for many of these bridge 'diseases'. Of course, there is no warranty with any of them, but they have been devised after a lot of thought by experts not only in North America but also around the rest of the bridge-playing globe.

The book is divided into three sections, each being devoted to a different aspect of the game: in turn, bidding, defense and declarer-play. And to give you a chance to exercise your own inventive minds, you may tackle some problems before reading each section. At the end of the book are sheets containing bidding hands that you may attempt with your favorite partner. If you get to the right contract every time, either you are already using the tools I suggest or they were suited to your own methods. The other two sections are prefaced with a prelude of problems. You may think about them and see if you can devise your own solutions. Whether or not you do, you can then examine my suggested 'answers'. After that, discuss them with your partner(s) and decide which (if any!) you would like to adopt. Even though I am sure you will not agree with everything I say, I do feel confident that if you utilize those ideas which appeal to you, your results will improve.

And now onto the first section, with its opening chapters concentrating on when to pass!

Section A
Bidding

Chapter 1

Speech is Silvern, Silence is Golden

Or as I might rather express it: Speech is of Time,
Silence is of Eternity.

Sartor Resartus, *Thomas Carlyle*

In the olden days, when methods were relatively unrefined, it used to be that the purpose of bidding was clear: to reach the optimum contract for your side. With the advent of super-precise scientific bidding methods, a great number of competitors learned how to reach the best spot and the pendulum started to swing back. The goal of bidding became twofold: to reach your par contract, and to disrupt the opponents' bidding machinery if it were their hand. A great number of ingenious conventions and gadgets were invented and used efficiently until the core of players became sufficiently familiar with them. The Unusual Notrump, preemptive jump overcalls, various preemptive opening bids at the two-, three- and four-level, two-suited overcalls, and so on, made their debut on the great bridge scene.

Let's face it, people *love* to bid. However, for all good things in life there is a price to pay; nothing is free. These bids work well against relatively inexperienced opponents, but often they draw a road-map for the declarer on the play of the hand. So the problem becomes when to interfere and when to keep radio silence because the enemy is listening.

As the non-playing captain of the Spingold team during the exciting 1985 Team Trials, I watched, enjoyed and often suffered through 256 boards, and, as you can imagine, I witnessed bridge played at the highest levels of competence and skill. First, I would like to share with you two of the challenging swing hands which highlight the problem under consideration.

Dlr: North   ♠ J 10 9 2
Vul: E-W   ♡ A 10 4 3 2
               ◊ 6 5
               ♣ A Q

   ♠ 5 3   ♠ Q 7
   ♡ Q   ♡ K J 8 7 6
   ◊ A J 8 4 3   ◊ Q 9 7
   ♣ K J 10 7 4   ♣ 9 8 2
               ♠ A K 8 6 4
               ♡ 9 5
               ◊ K 10 2
               ♣ 6 5 3

Table 1:

West	North	East	South
Stansby	*Meckstroth*	*Martel*	*Rodwell*
	1 ♡	Pass	1 ♠
Pass	2 ♣	Pass	4 ♠
Pass	Pass	Pass	

Table 2:

West	North	East	South
Bergen	*Pender*	*Cohen*	*Ross*
	1 ♡	Pass	1 ♠
2NT (a)	3 ♣	Pass	4 ♠
Pass	Pass	Pass	

(a) Unusual, showing length in both minors

At table one, after the opening lead of the jack of clubs and
a successful finesse, Eric Rodwell led the two of hearts. Chip
Martel, East, rose with the king and, seeing his partner's queen
drop, led back a low heart for Lew Stansby to ruff. Later, two
diamond tricks for East-West defeated the contract by one trick.

At table two, Marty Bergen led the queen of hearts. Forewarned by the bidding that this was likely to be a singleton, Hugh Ross rose with dummy's ace and immediately drew two rounds of trumps, playing West for a 2-1-5-5 shape. When the club finesse worked, declarer claimed his contract and a gain of ten International Matchpoints (IMPs) to the Grand National team.

Dlr: South   ♠ 8 6 5
Vul: E-W   ♡ K
              ◇ A 10 9 6
              ♣ K 9 8 5 2

♠ 7   ♠ J 10 2
♡ J 10 8 7 2   ♡ Q 5
◇ 4 3   ◇ K Q J 8 7 5 2
♣ Q J 6 4 3   ♣ 7

              ♠ A K Q 9 4 3
              ♡ A 9 6 4 3
              ◇ —
              ♣ A 10

Table 1:

West	North	East	South
Lair	Pender	Wold	Ross
			2♣ (a)
Pass	2NT (b)	Pass	3♠
Pass	4NT (c)	Pass	5◇ (d)
Pass	5♡ (e)	Pass	5NT (f)
Pass	6◇	Pass	7♠
Pass	Pass	Pass	

(a) Strong and artificial
(b) A positive response with clubs
(c) Roman Key Card Blackwood
(d) Four of the five 'aces'
(e) Do you have the queen of spades?   (f) Yes

Table 2:

West	North	East	South
Hamman	Meckstroth	Wolff	Rodwell
			1 ♣ (g)
Pass	2 ♣	2 ◇	2 ♠
Pass	3 ♣ (h)	Pass	3 ♡
Pass	3 ♠	Pass	4 ♣
Pass	4 ◇	Pass	4NT (i)
Pass	5 ◇ (j)	Pass	5NT (k)
Pass	6 ♡ (l)	Pass	6 ♠
Pass	Pass	Pass	

(g) Precision: 16-plus points and any shape
(h) Less than queen-third in spades
(i) Roman Key Card Blackwood
(j) One of the five 'aces'
(k) Grand Slam Try   (l) Two kings

Where Ross had to play in seven spades after an uncontested auction, he won the jack-of-hearts lead with dummy's singleton king, entered hand with a spade to the ace, ruffed a heart in the dummy, ruffed a diamond and tried to ruff another heart in the dummy, hoping East's queen had been a false card. However, Eddie Wold overruffed to defeat the contract.

In the other room Bob Hamman led the four of diamonds, Rodwell won in the dummy with the ace, discarding a heart from hand, and immediately drew two rounds of trumps, West discarding on the second round. The king of hearts, a diamond ruff in hand, a heart ruff in the dummy and a diamond ruff in hand with West showing out left declarer able to claim his contract. He ran his trumps to squeeze West in hearts and clubs, giving the Spingold team fourteen IMPs.

What can we learn from these examples? In hand one, Stansby preferred to be silent, proposing to enter the auction later if it seemed appropriate to do so, whereas Bergen judged to take immediate action. With favorable vulnerability, there would be no question of the advisability of overcalling straightaway; but with the actual setup it is less clear-cut.

In the second hand, Wold's discretion by not preempting despite his excellent seven-card suit paid off. He confided to me later that after a forcing two-club opener and a strong, conventional two-notrump response, he did not feel it was wise to tip off the declarer. As to the lead, he might have got a chance later in the auction for a lead-directing double.

Now for a hand from a less rarified atmosphere: the Mixed Pairs in the 1985 Fall Nationals in Winnipeg.

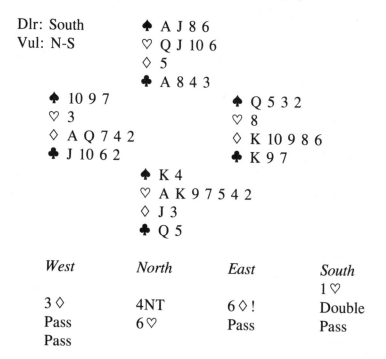

Dlr: South
Vul: N-S

♠ A J 8 6
♡ Q J 10 6
◇ 5
♣ A 8 4 3

♠ 10 9 7
♡ 3
◇ A Q 7 4 2
♣ J 10 6 2

♠ Q 5 3 2
♡ 8
◇ K 10 9 8 6
♣ K 9 7

♠ K 4
♡ A K 9 7 5 4 2
◇ J 3
♣ Q 5

West	North	East	South
			1 ♡
3 ◇	4NT	6 ◇!	Double
Pass	6 ♡	Pass	Pass
Pass			

Over my opening bid, West made a weak jump overcall that will not be found in any textbooks but which has become a regular occurrence in pair events these days. My wife, Edith, is an aggressive bidder, as can be seen from her immediate employment of Roman Key Card Blackwood. East applied the pressure with the jump to six diamonds, but we had our methods worked out. My double was DEPO indicating zero, two or four of the five key cards: the four aces and the king of hearts. Edith might have converted the double for penalties, knowing a key card was missing, but she likes to bid slams!

West led the ace of diamonds and switched to the three of hearts. I won in hand, ruffed my second diamond, made the Vienna Coup of cashing the ace of clubs and proceeded to run all my trumps. This was the position before the last one was played:

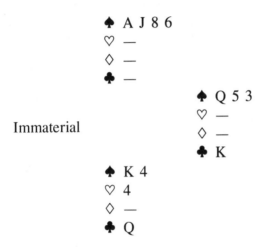

On the trump dummy's six of spades was discarded and East was unable to protect both black suits.

Have you noticed that I could have made the slam with an alternative line? I could have cashed the king and ace of spades before leading the jack. If East covers with the queen, dummy's eight is set up; whereas if he discards, I throw my club loser immediately.

Because of West's unwise preemptive jump overcall, I played East for the king of clubs *and* the queen of spades. If the opponents had remained silent I would have had to choose between the squeeze I played, taking a spade finesse or trying to ruff down the queen of spades in three rounds, perhaps having to fall back on a black-suit squeeze if West turned out to have started with queen-fourth in spades.

The path to success at bridge, especially in competitive auctions and even at the Olympian heights we considered first, is very narrow and scary. The close decisions are extremely difficult to judge and lots of points hang in the balance. However, here are some questions that you should ask yourself to try to resolve quandaries of this type:

1. Whose hand is it?
2. If it is theirs, may we have a profitable sacrifice?
3. By bidding, do I help partner with his opening lead?

My Tip for a Top

In potentially competitive situations, weigh carefully the risks of bidding versus the possible gains. Remember, speech is silvern, but silence may be golden.

Chapter 2

Discovery Through Passing

So let great authors have their due, as time, which is the author
of authors, be not deprived of his due, which is further and
further to discover truth.

Advancement of Learning, *Francis Bacon*

The concept of discovery plays was presented for the first time
by Terence Reese in *The Expert Game,* and since then it has
become a highly-valued tool in the repertoire of a first-class
card-player.

Discovery is defined in *The Official Encyclopedia of Bridge*
as: "The process of maneuvering the play in order to learn vital
information about the hidden hands."

Several years ago it occurred to me that parallel opportunities
may exist in some competitive auctions.

Nowadays everyone seems busy bidding preemptively in
order to put pressure on the opponents and to interrupt their
communications. The goal appears to be to deprive one's opponents of vital bidding levels. Alas, every action, every bid,
has its price. It is, of course, all right to jam the bidding and
to put the opponents to a guess when you have a good chance
of becoming the declarer. But if you end up defending, a competent dummy-player, by listening carefully, can often turn all
this extra knowledge to his advantage.

However, when holding certain hands with which you intend to become the declarer, sometimes aggressive and talkative
opponents should be given a chance to disclose further pieces
of information which otherwise might not become available.
If you know what your final contract is going to be, do not
need partner's cooperation and the opponents are in a forcing
situation, you may do best to remain silent instead of entering
the auction immediately. This will give the opponents every
opportunity to do you a favor by drawing a precise road-map
for your dummy-play. Here is an illustration of what I mean.

```
Dlr: West          ♠ Q 10 3 2
Vul: E-W           ♡ 6 4 2
                   ◊ 9 7 5
                   ♣ K 8 3
   ♠ K J 8 4                   ♠ A 9 7
   ♡ A 10 9 7 3                ♡ K Q J 8
   ◊ K                         ◊ J 10 8 4 3
   ♣ Q 6 2                     ♣ J
                   ♠ 6 5
                   ♡ 5
                   ◊ A Q 6 2
                   ♣ A 10 9 7 5 4
```

West opened with two diamonds, Flannery, showing a minimum
opening bid with four spades and five hearts; and East responded
two notrump, forcing to game and asking for further definition. Sitting South, I chose to sit back and listen. West rebid
three diamonds to describe his 4-5-1-3 shape (not the normal
Flannery response, which is three clubs), and East continued
with three hearts to see if his partner had anything more to add.
I was happy to continue passing, but when West bid four hearts
to say that he had done his all and it was passed round to me,
I felt it was finally time to enter the fray. It sounded as if they
would make four hearts, but that I could do well in my suit:
I bid five clubs.

West doubled, of course, and led the ace of hearts, under
which East signaled with the king. I trumped the second round
of hearts and immediately played a spade to the ten and ace.
East continued with hearts, I ruffed and led my second spade,
West going up with his king and exiting with a spade to dummy's queen, on which I discarded a diamond. Now it was easy
to play a trump to the ace, cash the ace of diamonds to extract
West's known singleton, run the ten of clubs, draw the last
trump and concede a diamond.

Only two down, and the opponents could make four hearts
with careful play even after a trump lead.

It is well known that two-suited overcalls like the Unusual Notrump and Michaels Cue-Bids often result in an opponent making a contract in which he probably would have failed after an uncontested auction because he knew so much more about the distribution. Here is an example, taken from the 1975 Mexican National Open Pairs.

Dlr: South
Vul: None

```
                    ♠ Q J 6 2
                    ♡ A K 7
                    ◇ 6 4 3
                    ♣ 9 3 2
    ♠ 8 7                           ♠ 10
    ♡ J                             ♡ 10 9 8 4 3
    ◇ A K 9 7 2                     ◇ Q J 8 5
    ♣ Q 10 6 5 4                    ♣ A 8 7
                    ♠ A K 9 5 4 3
                    ♡ Q 6 5 2
                    ◇ 10
                    ♣ K J
```

West	North	East	South
			1 ♠
2NT (a)	3 ◇ (b)	Double	Pass!
Pass	3 ♠	4 ♣	4 ♠
5 ◇	Double	Pass	5 ♠
Pass	Pass	Pass	

(a) Unusual for the minors
(b) A limit raise or better in spades

When East doubled three diamonds to show support for that suit, I decided to pass to try to find out more. Partner limited his hand with three spades, and East felt he had to have another bite at the cherry. I bid four spades, as I had intended all along, and West was persuaded to save: in fact a good decision as it is only one down. Now my partner, being unaware of the strength of my hand, doubled to try to stop me going on to five

19

spades, which was perhaps unwise with no honors in the minors. However, I wanted to play the hand.

West led the jack of hearts, an obvious singleton. I won with dummy's ace, drew the trumps ending in the dummy, East discarding a heart, and exited with a diamond to East's jack. He returned the ten of hearts, and after eliminating the diamonds I was pretty sure who had what. It seemed that West held the ace-king of diamonds, and so when I led a club from the dummy I rose with the king to make my contract.

On the next hand, from a local duplicate game, I was playing Precision, which I do sometimes instead of my Romex; and once more I was sitting South.

These were the four hands:

```
Dlr: South        ♠ 5
Vul: N-S          ♡ K 7 6
                  ◇ A K 9 6 5
                  ♣ K 9 3 2
   ♠ K J 10 6 2              ♠ 9 8 7 4 3
   ♡ 9 5                     ♡ 10 8 3 2
   ◇ Q J 10 3 2              ◇ 4
   ♣ 8                       ♣ Q 7 6
                  ♠ A Q
                  ♡ A Q J 4
                  ◇ 8 7
                  ♣ A J 10 5 4
```

West	North	East	South
			1♣ (a)
1NT (b)	Double (c)	2♠	Pass
3♠	4♣	Pass	4NT
Pass	5◇	Pass	5NT
Pass	6♣	Pass	7NT
Pass	Pass	Pass	

(a) 16-plus points   (b) Spades and diamonds
(c) A good hand with at least one of their suits

When East bid two spades I was happy to give partner a chance to double if he wished. And, as we are learning, perhaps West would have been wiser to pass. When partner indicated a club suit I used Roman Blackwood to discover he had one ace and three kings, and I decided to go for all the matchpoints. I was not proud of my final bid but felt that the knowledge of the opponents' hands made the risk worthwhile.

West led the queen of diamonds. I won with dummy's ace and cashed four heart tricks, discarding a diamond from the dummy. It was now a virtual certainty that West had at most a singleton club (with 5-2-4-2 shape he would surely have passed over two spades), so I crossed to dummy's king of clubs, finessed the jack and ran the clubs to squeeze West in spades and diamonds, dropping his king of spades at trick twelve to land the hoped-for top.

Perhaps the definition in the Encyclopedia should be modified to: ''The process of maneuvering the bidding and/or play in order to gain vital information about the hidden hands.''

Situations of this nature come up frequently, and the beauty of this approach is that it does not need partner's help; you play it solo. No partnership agreement is involved, and it does not depend on the system you are employing.

There are other situations in which this strategy of laying low may prove advantageous.

When you hold a long spade suit and do not intend to be outbid unless the opponents go overboard, there is no hurry to preempt; maybe if you go quietly you will be presented with useful hints as to the lie of the cards.

```
Dlr: North        ♠ 6
Vul: E-W          ♡ J 10 8
                  ◇ A 8 6 4 2
                  ♣ J 7 5 4
      ♠ 5                      ♠ J 9 3 2
      ♡ K 9 4 3                ♡ A Q 7 6 2
      ◇ K Q 10 9               ◇ 7 5
      ♣ Q 9 8 3                ♣ A K
                  ♠ A K Q 10 8 7 4
                  ♡ 5
                  ◇ J 3
                  ♣ 10 6 2
```

West	North	East	South
	Pass	1 ♡	1 ♠
3 ♠	Pass	4 ♡	4 ♠
Pass	Pass	Double	Pass
Pass	Pass		

When East opened one heart South decided to go slowly;
perhaps something good would happen. It did when West
showed a big heart fit with a singleton or void in spades yet East
was unable to express any interest in a slam. Now South bid
four spades, the contract he had always intended reaching; and
East judged well to double.

The opening lead was the king of diamonds. Declarer won
with dummy's ace and led the six of spades, finessing the ten
despite East's shrewd play of the nine. That gave South eight
tricks and an excellent score. Not a top, however, as some pairs
were defeating five hearts, two rounds of spades promoting a
trump trick for North.

Another common competitive situation occurs when an opponent cue-bids to show a good fit for his partner's overcall.
It is seldom right for the opener to double because this presents
additional bidding space to the adversaries. A discovery pass
will often provide one with important information.

In this hand from a national pair event I was playing with an expert but we were not a practiced partnership; and our opponents were first-class performers. I will set it as a single-dummy problem.

Dlr: South
Vul: None

♠ 4 3 2
♡ J 10 6 3
◇ A K 5 3
♣ 8 6

♠ 6
♡ A K 9 7 5
◇ Q 6 4 2
♣ K J 2

West	North	East	South
			1 ♡
1 ♠	2 ♡	3 ♡	Pass
4 ♠	Pass	Pass	5 ♡
Pass	Pass	Pass	

When East cued with three hearts I decided to make a discovery pass, and learned that West wanted to try for game. Not feeling confident we could beat four spades, I saved with five hearts. However, East was also unsure as to whose hand it was, so he passed it out.

West led the ace of spades and switched to the jack of diamonds. How would you have played from there?

The bidding had been most illuminating. They were holding only nineteen high-card points yet East had felt he was worth a three-level cue-bid and West had accepted the game-try, so they had to have some shape. I won the second trick in the dummy and immediately ran the jack of hearts. When that worked I drew trumps and returned to dummy with a diamond, East discarding a low club. Finally, it was easy to guess the clubs: East had to have the ace for his three-heart bid. I played a club to the king and escaped for one down, the full deal being:

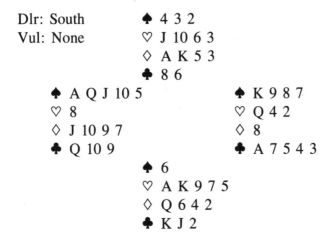

Dlr: South
Vul: None

♠ 4 3 2
♡ J 10 6 3
◊ A K 5 3
♣ 8 6

♠ A Q J 10 5
♡ 8
◊ J 10 9 7
♣ Q 10 9

♠ K 9 8 7
♡ Q 4 2
◊ 8
♣ A 7 5 4 3

♠ 6
♡ A K 9 7 5
◊ Q 6 4 2
♣ K J 2

This proved to be a good score as many East-West pairs made four spades, being able to guess the club suit after North's lead of the king of diamonds.

If West had settled for three spades over his partner's three hearts and I had been left to play in four hearts, I would have played for the trumps to be 2-2 rather than 3-1.

My final example occurred in one of our qualifying matches to select the Mexican teams for the 1986 Rosenblum Cup in Miami.

```
Dlr: West          ♠ 9 3
Vul: E-W           ♡ 10 5 4 2
                   ◊ 4
                   ♣ A 9 8 7 5 2
   ♠ 10 8                    ♠ A K Q J 6 5 2
   ♡ A K J 9 8 7 6           ♡ Q
   ◊ Q 8                     ◊ 10 3
   ♣ 6 4                     ♣ K Q J
                   ♠ 7 4
                   ♡ 3
                   ◊ A K J 9 7 6 5 2
                   ♣ 10 3
```

West	North	East	South
West	*North*	*East*	*South*
3 ♡	Pass	3 ♠	Pass
3NT	Pass	4 ♠	5 ◊
Pass	Pass	Double	Pass
Pass	Pass		

When East made a forcing three-spade response to his partner's preempt, I decided to sit back and listen for a round. However, when West suggested a quasi-balanced hand and East continued to four spades, it was time to come out of the bushes.

Because of the bidding I had no hesitation in dropping West's queen of diamonds and thus escape for two down, losing one heart, one club and two spade tricks.

At the other table South preempted immediately with five diamonds over three spades. Then he finessed East for the queen of diamonds and went three down, so my team gained five IMPs. Not a massive swing, but pleasing nevertheless. And note that the four-level is the limit for East-West as we can cash the ace-king of diamonds and ace of clubs.

I believe I have just scratched the surface of this promising tactic. I hope the enterprising reader will be encouraged to experiment with the idea, and that results over a period of time will prove its efficacy.

However, it is also necessary to sound a cautionary note. One can overdo this approach. One will encounter many situations where an early preemptive action will be imperative in order to stand any chance of receiving a good result on a board. For example, on the first hand of this chapter, if I had essayed an immediate four spades it would have been difficult for West not to bid five hearts.

Really, there is no substitute for judgment.

My Tip for a Top

If you have a long suit, especially in spades, and propose to become the declarer unless you are sure the opponents have overreached themselves, consider passing early on so that you learn more about the opponents' strength and distribution than you would by making an immediate barrage bid.

Chapter 3

The Little Black Box

A Persian's Heaven is easily made;
'Tis but black eyes and lemonade.
> Intercepted Letters, *Thomas Moore*

My favorite among the great bridge stories told by the former Lemac radio quizmaster Bob Hawk is the one concerning the little black box consulted by the most consistent winner in his game. Every so often, he would pause, peek into the box, close it without letting anyone else see its contents, and resume his winning ways.

When its owner died and his estate was auctioned off, that little black box proved to be one of his most substantial assets. Everyone who had played with him bid for that box. The person who eventually bought it proved once more that he often bid too much. When he opened the box he found that it contained a scrap of paper on which was written a single word: Pass.

In an endeavor to emphasize that it is folly to compete against good opponents with weak hands, I have written more than once (see Chapter 1) that "Speech is silvern, Silence is golden". This is especially true when your feeble 'chirp' has the twin disadvantages of encouraging partner to make the wrong opening lead, and of giving the declarer a road-map for bringing home his contract.

In the 1986 World Team Championship for the Rosenblum Cup in Miami, our underdog Mexican team upset the strongly favored Pakistanis in an early match, eliminating them from the knockout and consigning them to the Swiss; from whence, to their credit, they reemerged and reached the final, losing to the team of Woolsey, Manfield, Boyd, Robinson, Silverman and Lipsitz from the United States. Here is one board that contributed to Mexico's victory over the redoubtable Zia Mahmood and his team.

27

Dlr: West   ♠ A 9 8 2
Vul: None   ♡ K 6 3 2
                 ♢ A 4
                 ♣ J 5 4

♠ K Q J   ♠ 10 7 6 3
♡ 8 7 5   ♡ J
♢ J 10 8 3 2   ♢ Q 9 6 5
♣ A 2   ♣ K 10 9 7

                 ♠ 5 4
                 ♡ A Q 10 9 4
                 ♢ K 7
                 ♣ Q 8 6 3

Table 1:

West	North	East	South
Nisar	*Duran*	*Nishat*	*Mariscal*
1NT (a)	Pass	Pass	Double
Pass	Pass	2♣	Double
2♢	Pass	Pass	2♡
Pass	4♡	Pass	Pass
Pass			

(a) 11-14 points

Table 2:

West	North	East	South
Rosenkranz	*Fazli*	*Reygadas*	*Zia*
Pass	1NT (b)	Pass	2NT (c)
Pass	3♣	Pass	3♡ (d)
Pass	4♡	Pass	Pass
Pass			

(b) 12-14 points

(c) Transfer to three clubs

(d) Game invitation in hearts

At the first table, Nisar led the king of spades. The declarer, Laura Mariscal, won with dummy's ace, drew trumps and led a club to the jack and king. The diamond return was won in the dummy, and, with the opening one-notrump bid to guide her, declarer ducked a club. West's ace fell on air and the contract rolled home.

At the other table, we were not using the weak notrump, and my long suit was not one I wished to suggest to partner as a lead, so I rejected any thought of opening the bidding. And this worked well in the play. I led the king of spades, which Zia ducked. I could have beaten the contract now by switching to the ace and another club, but that was not easy to see, and in fact I continued with the jack of spades. Zia won with dummy's ace, drew trumps and ruffed a spade in an effort to get a count on the hand. Next came a low club to the jack and king. Reygadas returned the ten of spades, declarer ruffed in hand and I dropped the three of diamonds, an encouraging odd card. Zia crossed to dummy's ace of diamonds and played a club toward his hand. Assuming that, in addition to the three spade honors and something in diamonds, I could not have the ace of clubs, he went up with the queen and down one.

My Tip for a Top

As a guide when not to bid with borderline hands, I suggest that you pass when:

1. You do not really want to encourage partner to lead your suit.
2. Your suit is such that you do not really want to suggest it as a final contract denomination for your side.
3. There is little hope of your winning the auction and bidding will only help an enemy declarer's play.

Chapter 4

Don't be a 'Barefoot Optimist'

The optimist proclaims that we live in the best of all possible
worlds; and the pessimist fears that this is true.
The Silver Stallion, *James Branch Cabell*

We have a rainy season in Mexico between May and August,
and one afternoon during a particularly heavy downpour in 1986
I drove to our local club to pick up Edith, who was playing
in a duplicate with her regular partner, Maruca Cespedes. I
arrived during the last round and noticed that one of my favorite
characters, Godfrey Rawlins, was playing at table three. Godfrey is an Englishman who had grown up with Whist. Perhaps
because of this, he is a terrific card-player, his dummy-play
being flawless, bordering on the brilliant, and his defense im-
aginative. He is a natural bidder, preferring four-card majors
and no conventions beyond Stayman and Blackwood. That afternoon, though, he was playing with a pretty young partner —
Godfrey loves beautiful women — who had persuaded him to
employ five-card majors and Roman Key Card Blackwood.
Always deriving pleasure from watching him play, I decided
to kibitz Godfrey's last couple of boards.

Godfrey is what I term a 'barefoot optimist'. In a duplicate
his technical superiority makes him a regular winner, but at
the rubber-bridge table he would have to go without his shoes
to cover the losses caused by his bidding. He expects all finesses
to be on, all the suits to break favorably and partner always
to have the right cards for him.

When playing or defending at IMPs or rubber bridge it is
advisable — maybe even necessary — to assume the only lie
of the cards which allows you to succeed, but in matchpointed
pairs this is a very bad policy to adopt. Nevertheless, Godfrey
is a super-aggressive bidder, and even though his excellent

declarer-play usually produces one more trick than at other tables, he is often two levels higher!

Here are the two hands I witnessed. First of all, Godfrey, sitting South at unfavorable vulnerability, opened one heart in second seat holding

♠ A 7 5   ♡ A 10 6 4 3   ◇ 3   ♣ K Q 8 5

His left-hand opponent preempted with four diamonds, the pretty young North bid four hearts and East passed. With a twinkle in his eye, Godfrey bid four notrump. I was not sure whether the twinkle said that he had remembered he was using RKCB or that he was applying one of his favorite theories, to which I am strongly opposed, that when the opponents preempt, one has to gamble too. North responded with a disappointing five clubs, showing zero or three of the five aces, and Godfrey ended the auction with five hearts. (If North had had three aces, she would have bid on, of course.)

West led the ace of diamonds, and this was the full deal:

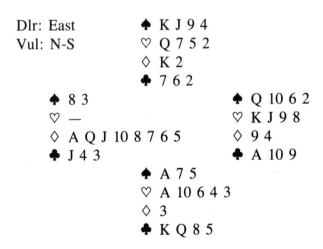

Dlr: East   ♠ K J 9 4
Vul: N-S   ♡ Q 7 5 2
                 ◇ K 2
                 ♣ 7 6 2

♠ 8 3   ♠ Q 10 6 2
♡ —   ♡ K J 9 8
◇ A Q J 10 8 7 6 5   ◇ 9 4
♣ J 4 3   ♣ A 10 9

                 ♠ A 7 5
                 ♡ A 10 6 4 3
                 ◇ 3
                 ♣ K Q 8 5

West switched to a spade at trick two, but with some help from East over which I will draw a veil, Godfrey managed to get out for one down, scoring an average when all the other declarers went down in four hearts.

He looked at me and said, "If partner has the same nine points but ♠ K x ♡ K Q x x ◊ x x x ♣ J x x x, I make five hearts if the rounded suits behave."

"Sure, Godfrey, but what do you need for six hearts? If your partner held ♠ K x ♡ K Q x x ◊ x x x ♣ A x x x, surely she would have bid five hearts over four diamonds."

Godfrey curled his lip at me in disdain; no use in arguing with you, George!

On the last hand my friend picked up

♠ K 10 8 3   ♡ A Q 10 5   ◊ 5   ♣ A Q 10 2

As dealer at favorable vulnerability, he opened one club. Given an uncontested run, the auction proeeded:

North	South
Pretty Young Partner	*Rawlins*
	1 ♣
1 ◊	1 ♡
3 ♡ (a)	4NT (b)
5 ♡ (c)	6 ♡
Pass	

(a) Limit
(b) RKCB
(c) Two aces but no queen of hearts

The opening lead was a trump, and this was the layout:

```
Dlr: South          ♠ A 7 4
Vul: E-W            ♡ K J 9 8
                    ◇ K J 9 8 6
                    ♣ 4
     ♠ Q 6 5                        ♠ J 9 2
     ♡ 7 4 2                        ♡ 6 3
     ◇ A 10 3                       ◇ Q 7 4 2
     ♣ K 7 6 5                      ♣ J 9 8 3
                    ♠ K 10 8 3
                    ♡ A Q 10 5
                    ◇ 5
                    ♣ A Q 10 2
```

As you can see, the club finesse lost (taken in an effort to avoid a spade loser), and even though Godfrey guessed correctly in diamonds, he still finished one down: a zero.

I got up to leave, but Godfrey shrugged his shoulders and commented: "I hoped partner's twelve points would be ♠ A x ♡ K J x x ◇ J x x x x ♣ K x. Sometimes Lady Luck is capricious."

It was no use telling Godfrey that there are far more minimum hands consistent with the bidding and maximum hands with most of their strength in diamonds that give no play for six than there are holdings which would bring home the slam.

We waited for the results. Maruca and Edith had won, three matchpoints ahead of Godfrey and the PYP. If it had not been for the last round . . .

My Tip for a Top

When the auction does not convey sufficient information, don't place specific cards in your partner's hand, but play him for the *weakest* holding consistent with his bidding. Only if there is still a chance for a good slam should you bid on.

Chapter 5

The Barefoot Optimist (reprise)

I am not an optimist but a meliorist.

George Eliot

A few weeks later, my telephone rang; it was Godfrey.

"Hello, George. I read your article about me. You really think I am a barefoot optimist?"

"Of course, Godfrey. I always write the truth. You are not offended?"

"Not at all, laddie; you just got the wrong picture about me. Anyway, I am back from safari in Nairobi."

"How was the hunting? Did you bring back any trophies?"

"Oh yes, I did well; and the bridge was good."

"Bridge? With whom did you play? The pygmies?"

"Oh no, there were some great players from Down Under in our party, and in the evenings these blokes even initiated me into the world of 'fertilizer' bids.

"Anyway, George, my date canceled for Sunday's duplicate; would you play with me? I am even willing to beef up on Romex."

"Oh no," I hastely declined. "I will be delighted to play a simple natural system with you."

"Ducky, I will prove to you that I am a solid bidder, no barefoot optimist, and to please you, we are even going to use splinter bids."

"But . . ."

"No arguments, please."

Sunday evening came around, and I met my suntanned friend, ready to go with convention-cards all filled out.

We got off to a flying start with a couple of good defenses, and then the usual fixes occurred. An atrocious trump break inspired a double of a cold four spades at other tables, but our timid opponent failed to double us. Godfrey even made five,

34

but we still scored well below average. And, on the companion board, they stopped in a partscore despite having 26 high-card points. The field, of course, was going down in three notrump.

Godfrey was not dismayed: "We will get them back."

I sensed storm clouds gathering, and the feeling of foreboding increased when, sitting North, I picked up this monstrous freak:

♠ A 10   ♡ —   ◊ K Q J 9 8 7 6 4 2   ♣ 4 3

The auction proceeded:

West	North	East	South
	5 ◊	5 ♠	Double
6 ♣	Pass	Pass	6 ♡
Pass	Pass	Double	Pass
7 ♣	Double	Pass	7 ♡
Double	Pass	Pass	Pass

West led the king of clubs, and this proved to be the full deal:

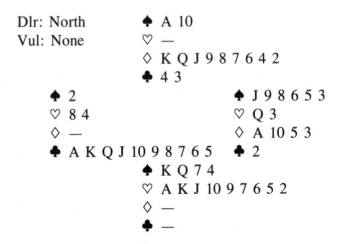

Dlr: North
Vul: None

♠ A 10
♡ —
◊ K Q J 9 8 7 6 4 2
♣ 4 3

♠ 2
♡ 8 4
◊ —
♣ A K Q J 10 9 8 7 6 5

♠ J 9 8 6 5 3
♡ Q 3
◊ A 10 5 3
♣ 2

♠ K Q 7 4
♡ A K J 10 9 7 6 5 2
◊ —
♣ —

My 'B.O.' ruffed the opening lead and ran all his trumps to catch poor East in a spade-diamond squeeze for thirteen tricks.

Godfrey gloated: "How about this old top? Didn't I bid and play the hand neatly?"

No use telling my dear partner that had West led a spade, there would have been no squeeze because my entry card would have been removed prematurely.

A couple of above-average hands followed. Then this gem came up:

Dlr: South
Vul: Both

```
                    ♠ Q J 10 9
                    ♡ Q 10 6 5 4
                    ◇ 7 6 2
                    ♣ A
   ♠ 8 4 2                           ♠ 7 6 5
   ♡ 8 7                             ♡ A K J 3
   ◇ A K 9 5                         ◇ 10 4
   ♣ 10 7 6 2                        ♣ 8 5 4 3
                    ♠ A K 3
                    ♡ 9 2
                    ◇ Q J 8 3
                    ♣ K Q J 9
```

West	North	East	South
			1 ◇
Pass	1 ♡	Pass	1NT
Pass	2 ♠	Pass	2NT
Pass	3NT	Pass	Pass
Pass			

West led the two of clubs, and South, looking at eight tricks in the black suits, needed only one from hearts or diamonds. The percentage play, of course, is to lead a low diamond from the dummy at trick two, hoping the honors are divided or both with East, and that the defenders cannot take three heart tricks.

Godfrey's play at trick two, however, was surprising: a low heart! East won with the jack and returned a club, Godfrey winning with the king and dummy discarding a diamond. Our

British friend calmly continued with the nine of hearts, and East won with the king. After some hesitation, he led another club, declarer winning with the queen and releasing a heart from the dummy. Accelerating his pace, Godfrey cashed the jack of clubs and four spade winners. A diabolical smile pervaded Godfrey's countenance: he led a low diamond from the dummy and put in the jack. West was endplayed: with only diamonds left he had to delight our optimist with the game-going trick in the suit.

Waiting for compliments on his tricky play, Godfrey commented: "Did you notice East's hitch after your three-notrump bid? I deduced that he wanted to double for a heart lead, then changed his mind. If that was the case, West figured to hold both diamond honors, so I took the bull by the horns and tackled the hearts myself. Obviously East was afraid to cash the ace of hearts, establishing two winners in the dummy. Table presence and psychology are more important than percentages. East's break in tempo gave the hand away."

With only two rounds remaining, my estimate was at least a 60% game. Then, with neither side vulnerable, Godfrey picked up as dealer

♠ —   ♡ K Q 9 6 4 2   ◊ A K 7 5 3   ♣ A K

The bidding went:

West	North	East	South
			Rawlins
			2♣ (a)
Pass	2◊ (b)	Pass	2♡
Pass	4◊ (c)	Pass	4NT (d)
Pass	5◊	Pass	7♡
Pass	Pass	Double!!	Pass
Pass	Pass		

(a) Strong, artificial and forcing   (b) Waiting
(c) Splinter bid — at least I remembered! (d) Blackwood

East's double, if I may paraphrase the Bard, "Had tongue at will and was ever so loud."

After a club opening lead, I tabled

♠ A K 3   ♡ 10 8 7 5 3   ◇ J   ♣ Q 7 5 4

There was no way for East to lose his ace of trumps, and we got what we deserved: a fat zero.

In spite of our score of 196 on a 156 average, we came in second, losing by two matchpoints.

"After your splinter raise and Blackwood response, I was sure you held the ace of trumps. Unlucky, wasn't it?"

I nodded with resignation, but I am not sure that my consenting gesture was convincing enough. Godfrey's last words echoed faintly in the distance: "Next time, George, we will play the Romex Grand Slam Force, I promise!"

Employing this convention, Godfrey would have bid five notrump instead of four notrump, and I would have responded six hearts, denying the ace of hearts. A six-club response indicates the ace or king of trumps, but not two top honors.

In case you are wondering, all these boards, including the incredible freak, were dealt by hand. But "next time" may not be until Godfrey buys a pair of tight shoes.

My Tip for a Top

Emphasizing what I said in the last chapter, remember that hope will not place in your partner's hand the specific cards you would like him to have. If your bidding cannot uncover all the information you need, lean toward caution.

Chapter 6

The Support-Showing Double

> What I want is men who will support me
> when I am in the wrong.
>
> *Lord Melbourne*

Life at the bridge table would be so easy if the opponents would not compete and you could find your best contract in an uncontested auction. Unfortunately, nowadays, particularly in duplicate tournaments, the enemy always seem to be in the bidding. They jam the auction, steal bidding levels and make you guess. Of course, there is no substitute for good judgment, but some new gadgets have been developed in the last few years to try to make life easier.

Here is an example of the awkward sort of position in which you might find yourself. You are playing in a matchpointed pairs event, and you pick up

♠ Q 8 3   ♡ A Q 10 5   ◊ J 6 4   ♣ K 5 2

Neither side is vulnerable, your partner opens one diamond and you respond one heart. So far everything is smooth sailing, but suddenly a wind gets up and makes the water choppy. Your left-hand opponent overcalls with one spade, partner raises to two hearts and RHO jumps to three spades. What do you do now?

If partner has four-card support, you are happy to take a shot at game. But what if he has raised with only three hearts? Now you prefer to double and collect the penalty. What is your guess?

Feeling most uncomfortable, at the time I decided to double; and was very relieved when the story had a happy ending, the full deal being:

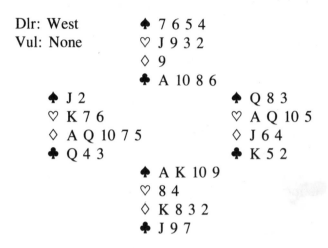

Dlr: West
Vul: None

```
                    ♠ 7 6 5 4
                    ♡ J 9 3 2
                    ◊ 9
                    ♣ A 10 8 6
   ♠ J 2                          ♠ Q 8 3
   ♡ K 7 6                        ♡ A Q 10 5
   ◊ A Q 10 7 5                   ◊ J 6 4
   ♣ Q 4 3                        ♣ K 5 2
                    ♠ A K 10 9
                    ♡ 8 4
                    ◊ K 8 3 2
                    ♣ J 9 7
```

We took five tricks and received a reasonable score as those pairs who attempted four hearts usually failed; though some declarers made game in hearts and notrump. However, exchange partner's four of clubs for North's two of hearts and we would have missed a game.

I was most unhappy being forced to guess like that and had started trying to find a solution when I heard from my teammates at that time, Jeff Meckstroth and Eric Rodwell, that a simple treatment could greatly facilitate the decision.

Whenever the bidding proceeds as follows:

West	North	East	South
	Opener		Responder
	1♣ / ◊	Pass	1♡
1♠	?		

a double by the opener shows three-card heart support, whereas a raise to two hearts (or higher) guarantees four-card support.

True, you sacrifice the penalty double of the one-spade over-call, but how often have you doubled one spade for penalties (with partner letting the double stand) in the last five years? And furthermore, all is not lost. Just as with negative doubles, partner with short spades may reopen with a double after hearing your pass if he feels you might have wished to double one spade for penalties.

Also, without the support-showing double, North has a difficult decision to make between passing and raising with three-card support after his right-hand opponent's one-spade overcall.

The double makes life more comfortable. Given the hand above, there are two possible auctions depending upon whether the opener indicates three-card or four-card heart support:

West	North	East	South
	1 ◇	Pass	1 ♡
1 ♠	Double (a)	3 ♠	Double (b)

(a) Three-card heart support   (b) For penalties

West	North	East	South
	1 ◇	Pass	1 ♡
1 ♠	2 ♡ (c)	3 ♠	4 ♡

(c) Four-card heart support

That was the initial basic concept, and it was so well received that it has been expanded by most experts. First of all, the strength of the double is not defined. It can be anything from a minimum up to a hand almost worth a two-club opening.

Obviously, with more than a minimum the opener takes another bid on the next round of the auction. For example, you hold

♠ 7   ♡ K J 4   ◇ A Q J 10 4   ♣ A K 7 5

and the bidding starts as before:

West	North	East	South
	1 ◇	Pass	1 ♡
1 ♠	?		

First of all, you double to show your three-card heart support. Now suppose that the auction continues:

West	North	East	South
	1 ◇	Pass	1 ♡
1 ♠	Double	Pass	2 ♡
Pass	?		

At this point, you follow up with three clubs to describe your shape and extra strength.

Secondly, the double is being used in all major-suit auctions in which the opener can raise partner at the two-level. So if you hold

♠ K J 6   ♡ 5   ◇ K J 10 4   ♣ A J 8 7 6

and the bidding starts:

West	North	East	South
	1 ♣	Pass	1 ♠
2 ♡	?		

a double shows three-card spade support because you could bid two spades to indicate four.

It is also possible to use the support-showing double in other auctions.

West	North	East	South
	1 ♣	1 ◊	1 ♡
2 ◊	?		

A double may be employed to reveal three-card heart support. Most experts have one exception, though.

West	North	East	South
	1 ♣	Pass	1 ◊
1 ♠	?		

Here a double shows four hearts, not three-card diamond support. (But, of course, you could agree with your partner to be consistent and play that the double does guarantee three diamonds.)

My Tip for a Top

Discuss these auctions with your partner and use a support-showing double when you think it will best serve you. It is a useful gadget that will often get you out of the guessing game highlighted at the beginning of this chapter.

Chapter 7

Continuing after Partner's Negative Double

Negative Capability, that is, when a man is capable of being
in uncertainties, mysteries, doubts, without any irritable
reaching after fact and reason.

Letter to G. and T. Keats, *John Keats*

The negative double — one of Al Roth's most brilliant con-
tributions to bidding theory — is acclaimed worldwide and used
by intermediate and expert players alike. However, few partnerships take the time to discuss the exact meanings of even
simple follow-up sequences.

To test your partnership understandings, consider this basic
sequence:

West	North	East	South
1 ♣	1 ♡	Double (a)	Pass

(a) Negative

Assuming partner's negative double shows *exactly* four spades
and at least enough points to compete at the one-level, what
would you bid now with the following hands?

1. ♠ Q 7 6 4   ♡ Q 8   ◇ A J 7   ♣ K Q 7 3
2. ♠ K Q 8 3   ♡ 5   ◇ 7 6 3   ♣ A Q J 8 4
3. ♠ A Q 6 5   ♡ K 7 2   ◇ A 4   ♣ A Q 7 6
4. ♠ A Q 6 5   ♡ 5   ◇ 7 6   ♣ A Q 10 7 5 4
5. ♠ A J 8 4 3   ♡ 5   ◇ 5   ♣ K Q J 8 4 3
6. ♠ A Q 10 5   ♡ 5   ◇ 7 5   ♣ A K J 10 5 4
7. ♠ A Q 8 6   ♡ K 6   ◇ 5   ♣ A K Q J 10 4

These are the answers I think you should have produced:

1. One spade. A minimum opening bid with four-card spade support.
2. Two spades. Saying that you would have raised a one-spade response to two-and-a-half spades! Around fifteen total points or six losers on the Losing Trick Count.

This is perhaps the most misinterpreted sequence by average players. The jump creates the erroneous impression of game-forcing values.

3. Two hearts. You force to game by cue-bidding the opponent's suit.
4. Three spades. A very strong invitation to game.
5. Four spades. You have a hand full of distributional offense in the black suits and no interest in defending.
6. Three hearts. A splinter bid with shortage in the opponent's suit and slam interest in spades.
7. Four clubs. A fit for partner's suit, solid or semisolid clubs and slam interest. Even better would be Roman Key Card Blackwood if you use it.

Well, how did you and your partner score in the test? If you had a high percentage, you have graduated onto more complicated topics. If you had problems, don't be discouraged: you are a member of the majority.

My Tip for a Top

There is no substitute for taking time to discuss bidding sequences with your regular partner; or, as my great friend and mentor, Johnny Gerber, used to say: An imperfect understanding is better than no understanding at all.

Chapter 8

Pulling Penalty Doubles

Half the failures in life arise from pulling in one's horse
as he is leaping.
Guesses At Truth, *Julius (and Augustus) Hare*

Have you ever discussed a seemingly obscure topic at great length with someone, only to have that feeling of *déjà vu* when you find a reference to the same subject in the morning paper? Or hurt your elbow on a door — probably still thinking about a hand in last night's duplicate — and in the crowded subway the next morning everybody seems to bump into your aching limb on purpose? I call this phenomenon the 'Sore Elbow Syndrome'. These events are no less or more frequent than normal; it is just that your mind is more aware than usual of these occurrences.

I notice a striking similarity when I decide to write an article about a certain topic. Trying to find good example hands, I ask my expert friends and I scan the literature, but often with little reward. Then, suddenly, as if by magic, the perfect illustration crops up at the table.

Some time ago I decided to pen a piece about the old bromide: Never take out your partner's penalty double. (Of course, none of us likes absolutes in bridge, or in life for that matter, so there may be justification to the saying: "Never say never.") There have to be times when it is correct to pull partner's double, but when? I was taught in my formative years that if I possessed a long, weak, unbid suit I should remove a low-level penalty double. Such a holding is only an asset on offense, not on defense; and partner might be expecting a trick or two from his top cards in the suit, but they will disappear because of your length. Notice that the emphasis is on *unbid*. If you have had

46

the chance to mention your suit earlier in the auction and *then* partner doubles for penalties, you had better sit tight. He has been forewarned; and it is good for partnership morale.

Within two weeks of deciding to write the article, the following hands came up. The first was in a knockout team event.

Dlr: North   ♠ Q J 9 7 2
Vul: Both   ♡ K Q 5 4
                ◇ 7
                ♣ A 5 3

```
        ♠ 8 6 3                    ♠ A
        ♡ 10                       ♡ A 7
        ◇ A J 5 3                  ◇ K Q 10 9 8 6 4 2
        ♣ Q J 10 9 4               ♣ 8 6
                  ♠ K 10 5 4
                  ♡ J 9 8 6 3 2
                  ◇ —
                  ♣ K 7 2
```

West	North	East	South
	Wold		Rosenkranz
	1 ♠	4 ◇	4 ♠
5 ◇	Double	Pass	5 ♡
Pass	Pass	Pass	

Not only was five diamonds cold but five hearts was also unbeatable, whereas five spades could have been defeated by a heart ruff.

Our opponents did well not to double five hearts, but perhaps they should have gone on to six diamonds: when in doubt, bid one more.

The other hand is even more dramatic in the sense that I bid my long suit for the first time at the six-level! It occurred when partnering Edith in our regular Monday evening club game.

This was the layout:

Dlr: North   ♠ A 10 4
Vul: Both   ♡ Q J 10 8 4 3
                 ◊ Q
                 ♣ A K 3

♠ K J 9 7 6		♠ Q 8 3
♡ 6 5		♡ A K 7 2
◊ A 9 3 2		◊ K J 10 5 4
♣ 7 5		♣ 2

                 ♠ 5 2
                 ♡ 9
                 ◊ 8 7 6
                 ♣ Q J 10 9 8 6 4

West	North	East	South
	1 ♡	2 ◊	Pass
2 ♠	Pass	3 ♡	Pass
4 ◊	Pass	5 ◊	Pass
Pass	Double	Pass	6 ♣
Double	Pass	Pass	Pass

As you can see, five diamonds doubled would have made, whereas the save in six clubs doubled was profitable, costing only 500. Rather fortuitous, but this result proved to be a top for us.

My Tip for a Top

Take out your partner's penalty double in competitive situations when you possess a long, weak, unbid suit.

Chapter 9

What is Forcing after Partner's Redouble?

> They
> Doubly redoubled strikes upon the foe:
> Except they meant to bathe in reeking wounds,
> Or memorize another Golgotha,
> I cannot tell.
>
> Macbeth, *William Shakespeare*

A surprising number of bidding disasters occur because one player thinks a bid is forcing, whereas his partner feels it is not.

A woeful letter from a correspondent who reads my articles in the A.C.B.L. *Bulletin* is eloquent proof of this point. It is a matchpointed pair event, neither side is vulnerable, and you are sitting South, holding

♠ K J 5   ♡ K 9   ♢ A Q 10 9 8   ♣ 8 7 2

You participate in the following auction:

West	North	East	South
			1 ♢
Double	Redouble	Pass	Pass
2 ♣	2 ♠	Pass	?

Your pass promised a full-weight opening bid, usually with some defensive values. What do you bid now?

My reader, thinking that the two-spade bid was non-forcing and devaluing his king of hearts, passed for a zero matchpoint score. Unfortunately, his partner held

♠ A 10 9 7 3   ♡ 6 2   ◊ K 2   ♣ A J 10 9

A raise to three spades would have been carried on to game and a respectable result.

Of course, there is a good case for doubling two clubs with that hand; but presumably East-West would have retreated into their nine-card heart fit, whereupon this hand introduces its spade suit and the game should be reached.

So, what is forcing after partner's redouble? These are the basic rules favored by most experts:

1. A new suit by the redoubler is a one-round force; with subsequent changes of suit or cue-bids being forcing to game.

2. The opener at his second turn should pass (or double with good trumps) with all balanced hands and with all full-value opening bids.

3. Any immediate bid by the opener, even with a jump, shows a minimum or sub-minimum opening bid in terms of high cards and primarily distributional values.

4. After a redouble and a pass or double by the opener to guarantee a sound opening bid, either the opening side plays the hand or the opponents play in something doubled.

The bidding begins 1 ◊ -(Double)-Redouble-(1 ♠). What would you bid with the following hands?

a. ♠ 10 7 6   ♡ K Q 4   ◊ A J 3 2   ♣ K 10 6
b. ♠ A J 10 8   ♡ 4   ◊ K Q J 8 7   ♣ K Q 3
c. ♠ 5   ♡ 3 2   ◊ K Q 8 7 6   ♣ A Q 10 7 6
d. ♠ 4   ♡ K 3   ◊ K Q J 9 8 7 4   ♣ Q 10 4
e. ♠ 3   ♡ 2   ◊ A Q 10 9 7 6   ♣ K Q 10 8 7
f. ♠ —   ♡ 8 2   ◊ A K 10 8 7 2   ♣ K Q J 10 4

In *a,* pass is correct. The hand is balanced and you would be happy to hear partner double one spade.

Next, double. You have four good spades and the penalty should be particularly satisfying if this becomes the final contract.

With *c,* bid two clubs. You have a minimum opening bid and two long minors. Give partner that message immediately. And you should make this bid even if RHO has passed rather than bid one spade. The opener must bid immediately if limited in terms of high-card points.

Holding hand *d,* you should jump to three diamonds. As the bid is made without giving partner a chance to double one spade, it shows a hand with a long, strong suit, good playing strength and little defense. In other words, something just too strong for an initial preempt.

Hand *e* has rather more in the way of playing-tricks than *c,* so you should jump to three clubs. This announces a minimum high-card count but good offensive potential.

Finally, hand *f.* I hope you passed. Any bid you make at this point will proclaim less in terms of high-card values. You should pass first and jump in clubs on the next round.

This last hand was part of a deal that occurred during a Mexican tournament.

```
Dlr: South          ♠ Q 10 7 4
Vul: Both           ♡ K Q 3
                    ◊ Q J
                    ♣ A 9 7 2
     ♠ A K J 3                    ♠ 9 8 6 5 2
     ♡ A J 10 9                   ♡ 7 6 5 4
     ◊ 6 3                        ◊ 9 5 4
     ♣ 8 6 3                      ♣ 5
                    ♠ —
                    ♡ 8 2
                    ◊ A K 10 8 7 2
                    ♣ K Q J 10 4
```

West	North	East	South
			1 ◊
Double	Redouble	1 ♠	Pass
Pass	Double	Pass	3 ♣
Pass	4 ♣	Pass	4 ◊
Pass	4 ♡	Pass	4 ♠
Pass	4NT (a)	Pass	5NT (b)
Pass	6 ♣	Pass	Pass
Pass			

(a) Roman Key Card Blackwood
(b) Two of the five aces and a void

South was minimum in high-card points for his pass and subsequent jump, but having only four losers he was clearly justified in adopting this strong approach. After that, North was always bidding at least six clubs as long as two aces were not missing.

There is one final point I would like to make. It is traditional in North America to play that a change of suit by responder over an opponent's take-out double is forcing at the one-level but non-forcing at the two-level. This must be borne in mind when the responder acts on the next round. If, however, you and your partner prefer the British approach that all new-suit bids are forcing, a redouble definitely announces a desire to penalize the enemy with a shortage in the opener's suit.

My Tip for a Top

Discuss with your partner and establish clear guidelines as to which bids are forcing and which are non-forcing after partner has redoubled over an opponent's take-out double.

Until the redoubler has limited his hand, any new suit by him is forcing.

If the opener indicates full opening-bid values, either the opening side plays the hand or the opponents play in something doubled.

Chapter 10

Lead-Directing Doubles
of Notrump Contracts

At church, with meek and unaffected grace,
His looks adorn'd the venerable place;
Truth from his lips prevail'd with double sway,
And fools, who came to scoff, remain'd to pay.
                    The Deserted Village, *Oliver Goldsmith*

A frequent cause of bad results in all forms of bridge is a misunderstanding between partners. Even longstanding partnerships are prone to such mishaps, usually because they have not been able to discuss thoroughly *all* the possibilities.

Let me show you two examples of costly misunderstandings with two different partners of mine. The first is from a duplicate game in Mexico City.

The opponents are vulnerable and you are West, second-in-hand, holding

♠ J 4 2   ♡ 8 6 5   ◇ A 9 8 7 5   ♣ 9 7

The auction proceeds:

West	North	East	South
			1 ♣
Pass	1 ♠	Pass	2 ♣
Pass	2 ♡	Pass	3 ◇
Double	Pass	Pass	3NT
Pass	Pass	Double	Pass
Pass	Pass		

What is your lead?

My partner, Miguel Reygadas, thinking that the double called for dummy's first-bid suit, led a spade, and the happy declarer wrapped up nine tricks. These were the four hands:

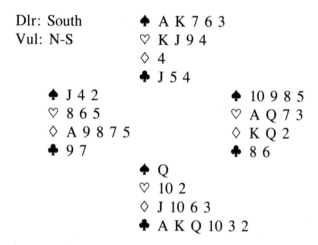

Dlr: South
Vul: N-S

♠ A K 7 6 3
♡ K J 9 4
◇ 4
♣ J 5 4

♠ J 4 2
♡ 8 6 5
◇ A 9 8 7 5
♣ 9 7

♠ 10 9 8 5
♡ A Q 7 3
◇ K Q 2
♣ 8 6

♠ Q
♡ 10 2
◇ J 10 6 3
♣ A K Q 10 3 2

As you can see, a diamond lead (or a heart) defeats the contract. I assumed that my double, following Miguel's double of three diamonds, called for a diamond lead.

This mishap reminded me of a tournament in Deauville many years ago in which I partnered, for the first time in my life, one of the top French players who has represented his country in many big international events. We were having a sensational game playing Acol, the English system, but lost first place on this hand.

Once more, only the opponents are vulnerable and you are West, holding

♠ Q 4 3   ♡ K J 10 8 4 2   ◊ 7 3   ♣ 5 2

The bidding goes:

West	North	East	South
			1 ◊
2 ♡ (a)	3 ♣	Pass	3NT
Pass	Pass	Double	Pass
Pass	Pass		

(a) Weak jump overcall

What is your lead?

I had no doubts which suit to attack. Assuming that the double called for the lead of my suit, I put the jack of hearts on the table and then watched helplessly as the declarer made his contract with an overtrick. This was the complete layout:

Dlr: South
Vul: N-S

```
                    ♠ A 10 8
                    ♡ 7
                    ◊ K 8 6 5
                    ♣ K J 9 8 7
  ♠ Q 4 3                         ♠ J 9 6 5 2
  ♡ K J 10 8 4 2                  ♡ 9 6 5
  ◊ 7 3                           ◊ 9
  ♣ 5 2                           ♣ A Q 10 6
                    ♠ K 7
                    ♡ A Q 3
                    ◊ A Q J 10 4 2
                    ♣ 4 3
```

Obviously my partner meant his double to demand a club lead. The sad thing is that without the double I would not have led a heart and we would have received a good score for holding declarer to nine tricks. Three notrump doubled and just made on a club lead would have been a little below average, but the doubled overtrick gave us a near-zero, and we had to be content with second place.

One could argue that if partner wanted a heart lead, he could have raised to three hearts rather than pass in the hope of being able to double a final contract of three notrump. But I prefer simple and clear-cut understandings. I play that when a contract of three notrump has been doubled:

1. If no suit has been bid (e.g. 1NT-3NT), the double calls for a heart lead (though I understand there is a case for partner to lead his shortest suit, or even a minor). This is called the Elwell Double, named after Joseph Bowne Elwell, who was born in Cranford, New Jersey, and who was one of America's top card players early in this century. He was a regular partner of Harold S. Vanderbilt.

2. If our side has not bid, the double asks for the lead of dummy's first-bid suit.

3. If our side has bid one suit, the double asks for the lead of that suit *unless* the partner of the opening leader was the one to bid the suit (see the next chapter).

4. If our side has bid two suits, the double asks for the lead of the suit bid by the opening leader.

5. If there was a Stayman auction, the double asks for the lead of the unbid minor (diamonds after normal Stayman, clubs after forcing Stayman). This is the Fisher double, named after Dr. John Fisher of Dallas, Texas.

My Tip for a Top

As these doubles are open to varying interpretations, discuss them all with your partner. To succeed at bridge, avoid misunderstandings.

Chapter 11

Lightner-Type Doubles of Notrump Contracts

Let the scintillations of your wit be like the coruscations of summer lightning, lambent but innocuous.
Sermon at Rugby by *Dean Goulburn*

In the last chapter I looked at the lead-directing meanings of penalty doubles of notrump contracts. The rules I suggested will work most of the time, but occasionally you will run into exceptional situations where that approach will fail.

Here are four awkward hands I witnessed either as a kibitzer or player. In each you are sitting East and must decide on your next action.

1. With neither side vulnerable and North the dealer, you hold

♠ A 5 3   ♡ Q 10 9 8 7   ♢ A   ♣ K Q J 10

The auction has proceeded:

West	North	East	South
	3 ♢	3 ♡	3NT
Pass	Pass	?	

2. With both sides vulnerable and North once more the dealer, you are looking at

♠ K 10 8 6 3   ♡ Q 4   ◇ A Q J 10 7   ♣ A

The bidding has been:

West	North	East	South
	2♣ (a)	2♠	3NT
Pass	Pass	?	

(a) Precision; showing at least five clubs and 11-15 points

3. At unfavorable vulnerability and your partner the dealer, you are surveying

♠ Q 10 9 4 2   ♡ K 3   ◇ 5   ♣ A K Q J 10

The action so far has produced:

West	North	East	South
Pass	1♡	1♠ (a)	3NT
Pass	Pass	?	

(a) Unfortunately, you are not playing Michaels Cue-Bids

4. Both sides are vulnerable and you have dealt yourself

♠ Q 5   ♡ J 10 7 6 5   ◇ 4   ♣ A K Q J 3

The bidding commences:

West	North	East	South
		1♡	1NT
Pass	3NT	?	

You can see what these four deals have in common. Every time you have bid a suit, the opponents are in three notrump, your partner is on lead, you have reason to suppose the contract will not make, yet only if he does not lead the suit you bid. To make matters worse, you know what is about to happen and are forced to watch helplessly as the declarer wraps up his contract, sometimes, adding insult to injury, with an overtrick or two.

Is there a remedy? The answer: a qualified yes. In all these situations you can use a double as an inhibitory Lightner-type double telling partner not to lead the bid suit, and informing him that you can defeat the contract if he leads the right *unbid* suit.

This is logical because normally partner will lead your suit, and the opponents will not normally bid three notrump without a sufficient holding in your suit. So doubling to tell him to lead another suit has a lot to recommend it.

Here are the full deals for the four hands given above. In every case you can see what a difference it makes finding the correct lead.

1.
Dlr: North
Vul: None

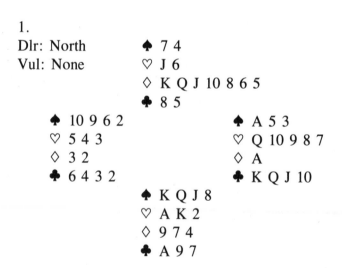

After the double, West should lead a club, not a spade, as East did not make a takeout double of the three-diamond opening

60

bid. But, of course, even a spade lead is good enough to defeat three notrump.

2.

Dlr: North
Vul: Both

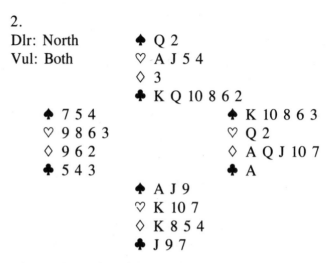

♠ Q 2
♡ A J 5 4
◇ 3
♣ K Q 10 8 6 2

♠ 7 5 4
♡ 9 8 6 3
◇ 9 6 2
♣ 5 4 3

♠ K 10 8 6 3
♡ Q 2
◇ A Q J 10 7
♣ A

♠ A J 9
♡ K 10 7
◇ K 8 5 4
♣ J 9 7

The double will elicit the desired diamond lead and collect a 200-point penalty. On a spade lead eleven tricks are there for the taking.

3.

Dlr: West
Vul: E-W

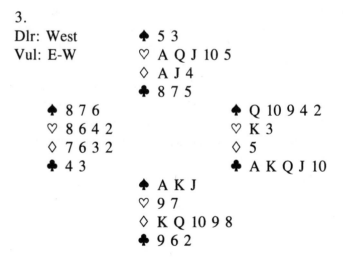

♠ 5 3
♡ A Q J 10 5
◇ A J 4
♣ 8 7 5

♠ 8 7 6
♡ 8 6 4 2
◇ 7 6 3 2
♣ 4 3

♠ Q 10 9 4 2
♡ K 3
◇ 5
♣ A K Q J 10

♠ A K J
♡ 9 7
◇ K Q 10 9 8
♣ 9 6 2

West has a problem over which minor to lead, but should go for clubs as that is his shorter suit.

4.

Dlr: East
Vul: Both

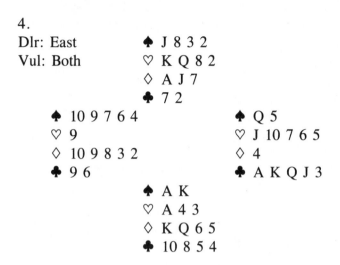

```
                     ♠ J 8 3 2
                     ♡ K Q 8 2
                     ◇ A J 7
                     ♣ 7 2
    ♠ 10 9 7 6 4              ♠ Q 5
    ♡ 9                       ♡ J 10 7 6 5
    ◇ 10 9 8 3 2              ◇ 4
    ♣ 9 6                     ♣ A K Q J 3
                     ♠ A K
                     ♡ A 4 3
                     ◇ K Q 6 5
                     ♣ 10 8 5 4
```

After East's double, West finds the killing lead of the nine of clubs. Spades and diamonds are unattractive because of the length held.

Taking a critical view of these lead-inhibiting doubles, you must ask yourself what price you are having to pay; what you are giving up. At IMPs the problem is not serious: you can no longer double when you know the lead of your suit is the killer, and the undertricks will be only 50 or 100 a time. But conversely you will defeat some contracts that would otherwise have made.

At matchpoints your gain may not be so obvious as many other pairs will be in the same boat as you; and less three-notrump contracts are bid with tenuous stoppers.

Of course, if the opponents step out of line and any lead will beat the contract, go ahead and double.

Finally, before giving this chapter's tip, did you ever see such an unsavory collection as those four West hands above?

My Tip for a Top

When the opponents have reached three notrump, you are the only person to have bid a suit for your side and your partner is on lead, a double bars the opening leader from attacking in that suit and demands an unusual lead from an unbid suit. With a choice between two unbid suits, the leader should usually go for his shorter holding. However, there is a warning: Handle with Care!

Chapter 12

Those Elusive Minor-Suit Slams

> We seek him here, we seek him there.
> Those Frenchies seek him everywhere.
> Is he in heaven? — Is he in hell?
> That demmed, elusive Pimpernel?
>   The Scarlet Pimpernel, *Baroness Orczy*

Of all slams, those in the minor suits are the hardest to bid, particularly in a matchpointed pairs event. Not only does one often have to leave behind the safe haven of three notrump while undertaking the adventure of exploring a slam in clubs or diamonds, but also it is easy to go overboard when using four notrump as an ace-asking bid. This is the reason why some diehard duplicate players go to the extreme of practically never bidding minor-suit slams at matchpoints. At International Matchpoint scoring, making five of a minor instead of four or five notrump is not a tragedy, but at matchpoints you may earn a near zero.

Johnny Gerber recognized this problem a long time ago when he proposed the four-club ace-asking convention that bears his name. But even if you are not in jeopardy of losing two aces, there is seldom enough room for further slam exploration with standard methods.

A simple idle bid put to good use may save you a lot of headaches and points. Four of a minor in game-forcing situations is practically never needed in its natural sense. With a group of experts, we started to use four-club and four-diamond bids after a minor-suit agreement in that suit as Roman Key Card Blackwood.

Here are some typical sequences:

West	East		West	East
1 ♠	2 ♣		1 ♡	1 ♠
3 ♣	4 ♣		2 ♦	4 ♦

West	East
1 ♡	2 ♦
4 ♦	

The final bid agrees the minor and is RKCB with the standard responses. And if you work it out, you will see that the response never takes you past five of the agreed minor, and allows you to use your normal methods for further exploration.

Here is a 25-point slam Eddie Wold, East, and I bid at a tournament in Puerto Vallarta using this method.

♠ A 5	♠ K Q 10 9 7 2
♡ A Q 8 4	♡ 3
◇ Q J 9 3 2	◇ K 10 8 7 5
♣ 8 6	♣ A

Opener	Responder
1 ◇	2 ♠ (a)
3 ♠ (b)	4 ◇ (c)
5 ♣ (d)	6 ◇ (e)
Pass	

(a) Long, semisolid suit asking partner to raise with a top honor
(b) I have a top honor
(c) RKCB in diamonds
(d) Two key cards and the queen of diamonds
(e) You have the right cards!

Here is another slam we bid from the same Regional.

♠ 6 4	♠ A K 8 5
♡ K	♡ A Q J 9 2
◇ A 8 7 6 2	◇ 10
♣ A Q 9 5 3	♣ K 8 2

Opener	Responder
1 ◇	1 ♡
2 ♣	2 ♠
3 ♣	4 ♣ (a)
4NT (b)	5 ◇ (c)
5 ♡ (d)	7 ♣ (e)
Pass	

(a) RKCB in clubs
(b) Two key cards and the queen of clubs
(c) Any kings? Five clubs would be a sign-off
(d) The king of hearts
(e) Fits like a glove

An excellent grand slam with only 30 HCP. The hearts were 5-2 and the ten was not dropping, so seven notrump did not make. Seven clubs only needed a 3-2 club break, with some additional chances.

An extra bonus with this style is being able to use four notrump by the RKCB bidder as a sign-off at matchpoints. Here is a good example from a club game:

Dlr: North   ♠ A Q 10 7 5
Vul: Both   ♡ K J 8
              ♢ 3
              ♣ Q J 8 7

♠ 9 6 4		♠ J 8 3 2
♡ 7 5		♡ 10 9 4 3 2
♢ A Q 8 6 4		♢ 9 7 2
♣ 9 3 2		♣ A

             ♠ K
             ♡ A Q 6
             ♢ K J 10 5
             ♣ K 10 6 5 4

West	*North*	*East*	*South*
	1 ♠	Pass	2 ♣
Pass	3 ♣	Pass	4 ♣ (a)
Pass	4 ♡ (b)	Pass	4NT (c)
Pass	Pass (d)	Pass	

(a) RKCB
(b) One or four key cards
(c) Stop here please
(d) OK!

After the opening lead of the six of diamonds, South won and played a club to East's ace. A diamond through allowed West to cash two diamond tricks, but North-South received a good matchpoint score for plus 630.

My Tip for a Top

After you have found a minor-suit fit and established a game-force, use the bid of four in the agreed minor as Roman Key Card Blackwood.

Chapter 13

Staying out of Trouble with Strong Hands

> They took me from my wife, and to save trouble
> I wed again, and made the error double.
>
> The Exile, *John Clare*

Bridge players are a funny breed; give them a powerhouse and they fall in love with it, bidding the spots off the cards they hold. It seems they feel a compulsion to broadcast to the audience every detail of their strength. So they are bound to get into more trouble with excellent hands than with weak ones as with the latter holdings — reluctantly — they have to stay out of the auction.

Here are two relatively simple hands on which Edith and I achieved unexpectedly good scores.

Opener	*Responder*
♠ K Q 10	♠ A J 2
♡ K 7	♡ 9 3 2
◊ K Q 8	◊ A J 10 7
♣ A K Q J 5	♣ 8 7 4

Only three pairs reached the optimal contract of six notrump by West. A popular score was six clubs made by West; and several went three down in six notrump by East, South leading the queen of hearts and collecting four tricks in the suit. Frequent sequences were 2♣-2NT-4NT-5♡-6♣ or 6NT and 2♣-2◊ (waiting)-3♣-3NT-4NT-5♡-6NT.

Opener	Responder
♠ A K Q 9 5	♠ 10 6 4 2
♡ K Q J 10 2	♡ 8 3
◊ 5	◊ K J 8 4
♣ A K	♣ Q J 10

Here we found that often the sequence of 2♣-2◊ (waiting)-2♠-3♠-4NT(RKCB)-5♣-5♠ led to an undistinguished contract that unluckily lost two aces and a trump trick, the spades being 4-0 offside.

The two-club opening for game-forcing or very strong balanced hands has been used for decades in a large variety of systems, yet the responses differ greatly and require careful handling. A method I have been using for a very long time and which has given me consistent results is to show controls immediately. Such an approach will tell you early whether a slam is possible or out of reach. Subsequent rounds of bidding are generally natural: five-card or longer suits are shown first; 4-4 fits can be explored later. Of course, this basic style can be beefed up according to your liking with a lot of gadgets: asking bids, splinters, and so on.

Here is the scheme of responses, with an ace counting as two controls and a king as one:

2◊ : No more than one control
2♡ : Two controls
2♠ : Three controls
2NT: Four controls in three or four suits: four kings, or two kings and an ace in a third suit
3♣ : Four controls in two suits
3◊ : Five or more controls

If responder gives the two-diamond negative and opener rebids two of a major, three clubs is a second negative.

Using these methods, this is how Edith, East, and I bid the above hands.

♠ K Q 10　　　　　　　♠ A J 2
♡ K 7　　　　　　　　♡ 9 3 2
◇ K Q 8　　　　　　　◇ A J 10 7
♣ A K Q J 5　　　　　♣ 8 7 4

Opener	Responder
2♣	3♣ (a)
6NT	Pass

(a) Four controls in two suits

The advantage of not bidding two notrump with four controls in two suits is evident, the slam being cold played by West. Whereas suppose the two hands were:

♠ A Q J　　　　　　　♠ K 10 2
♡ 9 7　　　　　　　　♡ K 3 2
◇ K Q 8　　　　　　　◇ A J 10 7
♣ A K Q J 5　　　　　♣ 8 7 4

Opener	Responder
2♣	2NT (a)
6NT	Pass

(a) Four controls in at least three suits

Once more, the slam is played from the right side.
　This was our auction on the second hand:

♠ A K Q 9 5   ♠ 10 6 4 2
♡ K Q J 10 2   ♡ 8 3
◇ 5   ◇ K J 8 4
♣ A K   ♣ Q J 10

Opener	Responder
2♣	2◇ (a)
2♠	3♠ (b)
4♠ (c)	Pass

(a) At most one control
(b) A reasonable hand with spade support as the second negative was not used
(c) Knowing we are off two aces

My Tip for a Top

To avoid trouble with strong hands qualifying for a two-club opening, try using control-showing responses. You may be surprised by the improvement in your scores.

Chapter 14

What's in a Name?

What's in a name? that which we call a rose
By any other name would smell as sweet.
                    Romeo and Juliet, *William Shakespeare*

For quite some time I have been receiving questions concerning the conventions that carry my name: the Rosenkranz double and redouble. Even more often I find them listed on the convention-cards of the opponents I meet at tournaments. Of course it is satisfying to the ego of any system maker to witness the popularity of one's brainchild, but the impact is marred by three facts:

1. my name is misspelled in every conceivable way;
2. the convention is constantly misused;
3. the A.C.B.L. is trying to remove names from conventions to avoid confusion when pairs employ different versions of the same basic method, so I had better rush this article into print!

In order to shed some light on this topic, let us start with the definition of the Rosenkranz double and redouble. They both represent a *raise* of partner's *overcall* from the *one-* to the *two-level* whenever right-hand opponent has made a forcing bid, such as a new suit or a negative double.

The distinguishing feature is that these bids *show* a top honor, the ace, king or queen, in the overcaller's suit; whereas the single raise denies holding a top honor, and is typically made with jack-fourth or worse support.

Here are some example sequences in which the final double or redouble *is* Rosenkranz.

	West	North Partner	East	South You
a.	1♡	1♠	2♣	Double
b.	1◇	1♡	Double	Redouble
c.	1♣	1◇	1♠	Double

In these, the final bid denies a top honor.

	West	North Partner	East	South You
d.	1♡	1♠	2♣	2♠
e.	1◇	1♡	Double	2♡
f.	1♣	1◇	1♠	2◇

And, as a corollary, the following sequences do not qualify for a Rosenkranz double.

	West	North Partner	East	South You
g.	1♡	1♠	2♡	Double
h.	1◇	1NT	2◇	Double
i.	1◇	1♠	1NT	Double
j.	1♠	2♡	3◇	Double
k.	1◇	2♡ (weak)	2♠	Double
l.			Pass	Pass
	1♡	1♠	2♣	Double
m.	1♣ (Precision)	1♠	2◇ (Non-forcing)	Double

In *g,* the opponent's two-heart bid is not forcing, so the double is responsive.

In *h,* RHO's raise is non-forcing, and the double is normally treated as for penalties after partner's strong overcall.

In *i,* RHO's one notrump is not forcing, so the double is either for penalties or responsive, showing the other two suits, depending upon which way you prefer to play it.

In *j,* the bidding is at the three-level. I play this double to show tolerance for partner's suit and five (or six) cards in the unbid fourth suit. Similarly in *k.*

In *l,* the two-club bid is non-forcing because RHO is a passed hand. As a consequence, the double is not Rosenkranz.

Finally, in *m,* as the two-diamond bid is non-forcing, the double is for penalties, not Rosenkranz.

Suppose you hold

♠ K 2   ♡ Q 10 5   ◇ K 4 3 2   ♣ 6 5 4 2

and the bidding starts:

West	*North*	*East*	*South*
1 ♡	1 ♠	2 ♣ / ◇	Double

this is *not* a Rosenkranz double (or, redouble, if East had made a negative double) as you hold only two cards in partner's suit. This is an honor-showing double.

My experience of the gadget shows that its value lies primarily in the area of defense, as exhibited graphically by the following two deals. The first occurred during the 1976 Vanderbilt.

```
Dlr: South        ♠ A 5
Vul: N-S          ♡ A 8 6
                  ◇ Q J 3 2
                  ♣ 9 5 4 2
    ♠ K J 10 9 2              ♠ 8 7 6 4
    ♡ 9 7                     ♡ K 5 3 2
    ◇ 7 5                     ◇ A 6 4
    ♣ J 10 8 3                ♣ 7 6
                  ♠ Q 3
                  ♡ Q J 10 4
                  ◇ K 10 9 8
                  ♣ A K Q
```

West	North	East	South
			1♣ (a)
1♠	Double	2♠	2NT
Pass	3NT	Pass	Pass
Pass			

(a) Precision: 16+ points, any shape

As partner's raise to two spades denied holding the ace or queen of spades, I avoided the otherwise seemingly natural spade lead, and elected to open the hostilities by attacking with the three of clubs. Declarer won and knocked out the ace of diamonds, partner returning a spade. Dummy won with the ace, declarer returned to hand and tried the heart finesse, but his luck was out and we cashed four spade tricks to defeat the contract by two.

At the other table West led a spade, my team-mate drove out the ace of diamonds and claimed nine tricks: two spades, one heart, three diamonds and three clubs. The swing was twelve IMPs.

The second deal arose during the 1980 Mexican trials.

```
Dlr: North          ♠ Q 10 7 5
Vul: Both           ♡ 10 6
                    ◊ Q J 9 5
                    ♣ A 7 4
     ♠ A 4 2                    ♠ 9 8
     ♡ A Q 7 5 3                ♡ K J 4 2
     ◊ 3                        ◊ 7 4 2
     ♣ J 10 8 6                 ♣ Q 5 3 2
                    ♠ K J 6 3
                    ♡ 9 8
                    ◊ A K 10 8 6
                    ♣ K 9
```

West	North	East	South
Rosenkranz		*Dubson*	
			1 ◊
1 ♡	Double	Redouble	1 ♠
3 ♡	3 ♠	Pass	4 ♠
Double	Pass	Pass	Pass

As my partner's double indicated the king of hearts and I held the ace of trumps and a side-suit singleton, I was able to visualize the fatal diamond ruff. I led the three of diamonds, declarer won in hand and led a trump, but I hopped up with the ace and led a heart. To my agreeable surprise, partner won this with the jack and gave me the diamond ruff. Underleading my heart honors for the second time, I received a second ruff and we collected 500.

On a heart lead and continuation, our team-mates made four spades for a swing of fifteen IMPs.

By way of a postscript, recently my regular partner Eddie Wold has been enjoying considerable success with the Reverse Rosenkranz Double and Redouble. A raise of partner's suit *promises* a top honor, whereas a double or redouble denies an honor.

The logic behind this is that you are more likely to want to contest the partscore on a borderline hand when you hold a fitting honor than when you do not.

This seems a sensible variation to me, but another proposal made by other players that the convention be employed with raises to the three-level is more questionable. I am not in favor of this change.

My Tip for a Top

When intending to use a new convention, learn about its exact scope. Bid practice hands in advance of using it at the table so as to feel comfortable with it.

Section B
Defense

The Prelude

What is the answer? . . . In that case, what is the question?
The Last Words of *Gertrude Stein*

1. Given that no special conditions exist, which order of priority would you assign to the three possible signals: attitude, count and suit preference? (Page 86)

2.
Dlr: East   ♠ Q J
Vul: E-W   ♡ A J 9
               ◊ Q J 7
               ♣ 10 7 5 4 2
                              ♠ 10 9 6 4
                              ♡ 7 3
                              ◊ K 10 5 4 3
                              ♣ Q 3

West	North	East	South
		Pass	1 ♡
Pass	1NT (a)	Pass	2 ♡
Pass	3 ♡	Pass	4 ♡
Pass	Pass	Pass	

(a) Forcing

Partner leads the king of clubs, and you drop the three. Next partner cashes the ace of diamonds. With which card do you signal this time? (Page 88)

3.

Dlr: West	♠ A J 7 3		
Vul: E-W	♡ J 9 6 4 2		
	◇ Q		
	♣ A K Q		

♠ —
♡ A 10 7
◇ A K J 5 4
♣ J 10 8 4 2

West	North	East	South
1 ◇	Double	Pass	2 ♠
Pass	4 ♠	Pass	Pass
Pass			

You lead the king of diamonds and declarer contributes the seven. What do you do at trick two if partner plays (i) the ten, (ii) the eight, or (iii) the two? (Page 95)

4.

Dlr: South	♠ 6 5 4 2		
Vul: Both	♡ A Q 10 2		
	◇ A 6 3		
	♣ A 6		

♠ K 9 7 3
♡ —
◇ J 9 7 4
♣ J 9 7 3 2

West	North	East	South
			1 ♡
Pass	3 ♡ (a)	Pass	4 ♡
Pass	Pass	Pass	

(a) Forcing

You lead the two of clubs, low from odd, dummy contributes the six, partner plays the queen and declarer wins with the king. While trumps are being drawn, partner proving to have started with jack-fourth, what are your discards? (Page 106)

5.
Dlr: South
Vul: E-W

♠ Q 10 7 6 2
♡ 10 8 2
♦ 7
♣ Q 8 6 2

♠ 5
♡ Q 9 7 4
♦ A Q J 9 8
♣ J 7 5

West	North	East	South
			2NT
Pass	3♡ (a)	Pass	3♠
Pass	3NT	Pass	Pass
Pass			

(a) Transfer bid

Partner leads the two of diamonds (in principle, fourth best), dummy contributes the seven, you put in the jack and declarer wins with the king. He continues with the ace and another spade to West's king. Partner continues with the four of diamonds; how do you defend? (Page 110)

6.

Dlr: East
Vul: E-W

♠ 9 8 7 5
♡ Q 7 2
◇ 9 6 5
♣ K 10 2

♠ 6 4 3 2
♡ A K 4 3
◇ K 7 2
♣ 5 4

West	North	East	South
		Pass	1NT
Pass	Pass	Double (a)	Pass
Pass	Pass		

(a) Showing a club suit

You lead the five of clubs, dummy's ten is put in, and partner's jack holds the trick. He switches to the queen of diamonds, which wins. What would you do if partner continues with (a) the jack or (b) the ten of diamonds, declarer putting up the ace?

(Page 113)

7.

Dlr: South
Vul: Both

♠ A J 10 5 2
♡ J
◇ K J 10
♣ J 8 6 4

♠ 9
♡ A 10 8 2
◇ 9 8 6 3
♣ Q 9 7 5

West	North	East	South
			1 ◇
Pass	1 ♠	Pass	2NT
Pass	3NT	Pass	Pass
Pass			

You lead the two of hearts and declarer wins partner's queen with his king. South immediately tries the spade finesse, but East wins with the king and returns the seven of hearts. What do you do when declarer plays the five? Would it make a difference if partner played back the four of hearts?

(Page 117)

8.

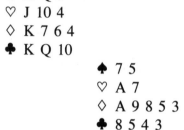

♠ K Q 3
♡ J 10 4
◇ K 7 6 4
♣ K Q 10

♠ 7 5
♡ A 7
◇ A 9 8 5 3
♣ 8 5 4 3

West	North	East	South
			1 ♠
Pass	2NT	Pass	3 ♣
Pass	3 ♠	Pass	4 ♠
Pass	Pass	Pass	

Partner leads the three of hearts, fourth best, and you win with the ace, declarer playing the five. Plan the defense.

(Page 140)

Chapter 1

Signals Anyone?

Ships that pass in the night, and speak each other
 in passing;
Only a signal shown and a distant voice in the
 darkness;
So on the ocean of life we pass and speak one another,
Only a look and a voice; then darkness again and a
 silence.

The Theologian's Tale, *Henry Wadsworth Longfellow*

Defense in bridge — the most difficult part of the game — is a partnership undertaking and therefore must be based on communication. The only legal way to achieve this is through signals which hinge on the size and order of the cards played by each defender. The great French player and theorist, Claude Delmouly, calls this the language of the cards.

The shady side of bridge history conserves in its annals various instances of illegal signaling, but I prefer to forget about them and instead to recount a true humorous incident which occurred many years ago, just after the Alert procedure had been introduced. Playing in a national women's pair event with Alicia Duran, my wife, Edith, became the declarer in a suit contract against two amiable ladies. As soon as the opening lead was made, Edith's right-hand opponent said: "Alert!"

Puzzled by this unusual warning, an inquiry elicited this striking explanation: "My partner has just led a singleton."

"But how can you tell?" was the incredulous question.

"Look at our convention card; it states that singletons are led with the left hand, and my partner just did so."

Of course, the Director was called but he had a hard time explaining to the women that their approach was not an approved convention.

After the defense has struck its only advantageous blow in the form of the opening lead, cooperation begins and signaling should start. I recommend the classical order of priority for signals well described in the bridge literature, in particular by Kantar, Woolsey and Stewart. These are: (i) attitude, (ii) count, and (iii) suit preference. When the first, attitude, is known, an automatic shift takes place to the second, count. After that is completed or already disclosed, the last remaining signal follows.

In this chapter I do not intend to deal with the mechanics of *how* to signal, leaving it to the reader to select his favorite method: normal, upside-down or odd-even, to name the most commonly employed. However, for the sake of clarity, let us stress some important general principles, even if they appear to be well known. Signals take place in three different circumstances: on partner's lead, on declarer's lead, and discarding on a suit led by either partner or declarer. All signals are on in the first case; in the second, attitude is practically always clear, so, if it cannot help declarer more than partner, we switch to the second and third gears for count and suit preference; and on discards all three are possible.

Enough of theory for the moment. As the Chinese saying goes, one picture is worth a thousand words; so let us look at this hand from the Board-a-Match Teams at the 1986 Fall Nationals in Atlanta.

```
Dlr: East          ♠ Q J
Vul: E-W           ♡ A J 9
                   ◇ Q J 7
                   ♣ 10 7 5 4 2
      ♠ 8 7 5                      ♠ 10 9 6 4
      ♡ 8 2                        ♡ 7 3
      ◇ A 9 8 2                    ◇ K 10 5 4 3
      ♣ A K J 9                    ♣ Q 3
                   ♠ A K 3 2
                   ♡ K Q 10 6 5 4
                   ◇ 6
                   ♣ 8 6
```

West	North	East	South
Freed		*Passell*	
		Pass	1 ♡
Pass	1NT (a)	Pass	2 ♡
Pass	3 ♡	Pass	4 ♡
Pass	Pass	Pass	

(a) Forcing

Defending against four hearts, Gene Freed led the king of
clubs, and East dropped the three. Freed switched to the ace
of diamonds. Realizing that his partner, holding two aces and
a king, would have overcalled with a five-card minor, Mike
Passell, despite holding the king of diamonds, played a
discouraging three. West now cashed his ace of clubs, holding
declarer to ten tricks, whereas a diamond continuation would
have let the eleventh trick through. A great example of
cooperative signaling: the player with the vital piece of information, East above, makes the critical play, steering his partner to the winning defense. And along with Mark Lair, Ed Manfield and Kit Woolsey, they won the event.

Let us look at a relatively simple but frequently occurring
situation:

Dummy
♡ J 8 **6**

You   *Partner*
♡ **K** Q 10 4   ♡ **2**

Declarer
♡ **5**

You lead the king of hearts, partner contributes the two and declarer the five. What is the significance of partner's play?

Declarer surely cannot have the ace as he would have won the trick, proposing to promote the jack later in the play. Is the two an attitude signal, asking for a switch? By no means. In this case, East knows that West will know he has the ace once the king holds the trick, so moving one step down the signaling priority ladder, the two must be a count signal, indicating an odd number of cards in the suit (assuming normal signals).

Alas, bridge is not always so simple. This deal occurred during the Open Pairs in the 1980 European Pairs Championships in Monte Carlo.

Dlr: South   ♠ A 9 8 6
Vul: None   ♡ 10 6 2
               ♦ A 5 2
               ♣ J 8 6

♠ J 3		♠ 10 4 2
♡ K Q 7		♡ A J 5 4
♦ 9 7 4 3		♦ 10 8 6
♣ K Q 10 3		♣ 5 4 2

            ♠ K Q 7 5
            ♡ 9 8 3
            ♦ K Q J
            ♣ A 9 7

West	North	East	South
			1NT
Pass	3NT	Pass	Pass
Pass			

Three notrump was an ambitious contract, apparently standing
no chance against good defense. However, two French inter-
nationals, Albert Faigenbaum and Jean-Marc Roudinesco, found
a successful deceptive play. When West led the king of clubs,
they both allowed him to hold the trick! Assuming that partner
held the ace, both Wests continued with a low club, handing
the declarers their 'impossible' contract.

Attitude or count first has been the subject of long-lasting
debates between different schools of theorists. Earlier, I indicated my preference for attitude taking precedence over count.
However, there is one situation in which the order of priority
should be reversed: when the opening lead is a high honor from
a long suit, dummy shows up with more than one card in the
suit and the contract is at the five- or six-level. In this case,
count should be given by third hand. This is imperative because
the defense have to know how many cashable tricks are available

in their long suit. Similar considerations apply when the opening leader has made a preemptive bid or otherwise shown length.

Here are two examples from the 1981 Mexican Trials.

Dlr: West
Vul: N-S

```
                    ♠ 9 5
                    ♡ A 10 5 2
                    ◊ 10 7
                    ♣ J 10 5 4 3
     ♠ A K J 7 6 2              ♠ Q 10 4 3
     ♡ 4                        ♡ 7 6
     ◊ Q 9 8                    ◊ K J 6 5 2
     ♣ K 9 8                    ♣ 6 2
                    ♠ 8
                    ♡ K Q J 9 8 3
                    ◊ A 4 3
                    ♣ A Q 7
```

West	North	East	South
Dubson		Rosenkranz	
1 ♠	Pass	2 ♠	3 ♡
3 ♠	4 ♡	Pass	Pass
4 ♠	Pass	Pass	5 ♡
Pass	Pass	Pass	

Sol Dubson led the king of spades and I gave count by dropping the ten. Knowing that I had an even number and that declarer would ruff the second round, Dubson looked for a useful shift and led the eight of diamonds. This turned out to be the killer as any other play would have allowed declarer to establish his club suit after drawing the outstanding trumps and divest himself of his diamond losers. And that is exactly what happened at the other table, giving our team thirteen IMPs.

In the second half of the match, a similar situation produced another favorable swing.

```
Dlr: West           ♠ 6 2
Vul: N-S            ♡ K Q J 6
                    ◊ A Q 7 4
                    ♣ K J 10
    ♠ A K Q 10 9 8 4        ♠ J 3
    ♡ 7                     ♡ 8 4 3
    ◊ 6 5                   ◊ K J 8 3 2
    ♣ 9 5 2                 ♣ 8 7 6
                    ♠ 7 5
                    ♡ A 10 9 5 2
                    ◊ 10 9
                    ♣ A Q 4 3
```

West	North	East	South
Dubson		*Rosenkranz*	
4♠	Double	Pass	5♡
Pass	Pass	Pass	

Dubson led the queen of spades and I signaled with the jack, showing a singleton or doubleton. Dubson knew he could cash a second spade trick; and declarer eventually lost a diamond to end one down.

At the other table East, playing attitude signals, dropped the three of spades at trick one, hoping for a diamond shift. His partner found the switch, but declarer hopped up with the ace, drew trumps and discarded dummy's spade loser on the fourth round of clubs.

While giving count on declarer's lead is often the right thing to do, any time the information can only help the declarer, you should refrain from signaling. This is a common situation:

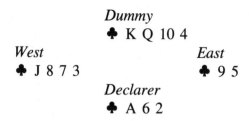

Dummy
♣ K Q 10 4

West
♣ J 8 7 3

East
♣ 9 5

Declarer
♣ A 6 2

Declarer plays a club to the king, one back to his ace and a third round. If both West and East have echoed to show an even number and declarer believes them, he will collect four tricks in the suit.

Here, the defenders do best not to signal; or to take up a suggestion made by Jerold A. Fink in an article published in the July 1986 issue of *The Bridge World.* He proposed 'cloaking' the count by considering only the low cards accompanying the finessable honor. Here, West shows an odd number of cards and East an even number, but from the declarer's point of view the suit is distributed either as above or is breaking 3-3; he cannot tell which.

Our next topic is the suit preference signal. One of the problems inexperienced partnerships encounter is interpreting when a signal is suit preference rather than attitude or count. But if correctly used, the suit preference signal is a powerful tool. Apart from the well-known situations involving regaining the lead after giving partner a ruff, here is a position that occurs frequently.

Dummy
◊ K Q 10 8 5

You
◊ A 7 3

Partner
◊ 9 4 2

Declarer
◊ J 6

Playing in notrump, dummy has no side entry, declarer wins

a trick and leads the jack of diamonds. You duck, of course, and partner drops the two to show an odd number of diamonds. When declarer continues with the six, you rise with the ace (if declarer has four diamonds, you cannot kill the suit anyway) and partner has the chance for a suit preference signal. If he plays the nine, he is indicating a holding in a higher-ranking suit. If, however, he drops the four he may want the lower-ranking suit or he may have no particular preference.

Here is another situation in which the suit preference signal occurs. It cropped up during the Men's Pairs in the 1981 Mexican Nationals.

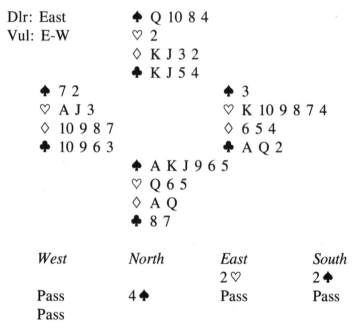

Dlr: East ♠ Q 10 8 4
Vul: E-W ♡ 2
     ♢ K J 3 2
     ♣ K J 5 4

♠ 7 2   ♠ 3
♡ A J 3   ♡ K 10 9 8 7 4
♢ 10 9 8 7   ♢ 6 5 4
♣ 10 9 6 3   ♣ A Q 2

     ♠ A K J 9 6 5
     ♡ Q 6 5
     ♢ A Q
     ♣ 8 7

West	North	East	South
		2 ♡	2 ♠
Pass	4 ♠	Pass	Pass
Pass			

West led the ace of hearts but could not be sure whether it was better to switch at trick two to clubs or diamonds. However, East rode to the rescue, contributing the four as a suit preference signal for clubs. The club switch held declarer to ten tricks and an above-average board. Note that if East had wanted a diamond switch, he would have signaled with the ten of hearts.

And to complete this subject, if under different circumstances (perhaps for a trump promotion or fearing any switch) East wanted hearts to be continued at trick two despite dummy's singleton, he would have played a middle spot-card.

This deal, another on the same theme, is taken from Kit Woolsey's excellent book, *Partnership Defense*.

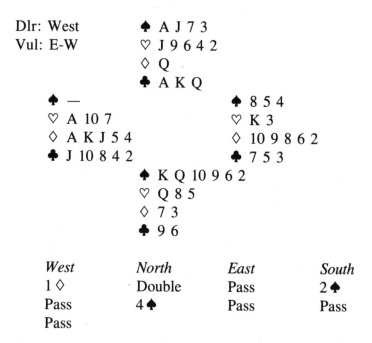

Dlr: West
Vul: E-W

♠ A J 7 3
♡ J 9 6 4 2
◇ Q
♣ A K Q

♠ —
♡ A 10 7
◇ A K J 5 4
♣ J 10 8 4 2

♠ 8 5 4
♡ K 3
◇ 10 9 8 6 2
♣ 7 5 3

♠ K Q 10 9 6 2
♡ Q 8 5
◇ 7 3
♣ 9 6

West	North	East	South
1 ◇	Double	Pass	2 ♠
Pass	4 ♠	Pass	Pass
Pass			

What should West lead after winning the first trick with the king of diamonds? Playing the suggested methods given above, East will drop the ten at trick one to indicate a heart card. And if West underleads his ace of hearts at trick two, four spades is defeated.

Before moving on, if you use the Italian odd-even signals*, an odd card would request a diamond continuation, and a high

---

*At the time of writing, in 1987, the A.C.B.L. has made odd-even signals illegal, permitting only odd-even discards. This move seems wrong to me, and I hope the light will be seen and the signals reinstated in the not too distant future.

even card would indicate a heart switch. My partner, Miguel Reygadas, has an additional twist: Playing an honor at trick one asks for a trump switch. Counting the ten as an honor, in the above example, East would play the eight of diamonds at trick one to ask for the heart switch.

This is such a fascinating subject that I tried to get a broader perspective by interviewing a number of the top American players. I found a general agreement with my own notions.

They all feel that advancing players should use signals practically all the time because, in order to become a good defender, they have to learn to count; and for counting, signals are necessary. Also, the experts think that signals should always be made at trick one; and that it normally pays to signal virtually all the time when playing in a weak field or in a large matchpointed pair event as few opponents will be playing much attention.

However, at the expert level the opinions begin to diverge. The question becomes not so much *how* to signal but *when, whether* and *how frequently*. Interestingly, the answer depends, as Edgar Kaplan pointed out, on the temperament of the expert. At one end of the spectrum came Barry Crane who insisted on always being given the count. He was convinced that he could make better use of the information communicated and did not care about the declarer being told too. At the other extreme comes Al Roth, who I am told instructs his partners not to tell him what he already knows!

The late B. J. Becker also believed in signaling the count almost all the time, arguing that it saves time and energy which can be put to better use.

As to the rest, there is hardly an American expert who does not give an attitude signal at trick one. But from here on I can distinguish three schools, which I shall call the ultramoderns, the freelancers and, if they will forgive the label, the old-timers. Though no expert will quarrel with the concept of telling partner as much as is necessary and declarer as little as possible, the question arises of how to achieve this. Are there any rules or is this 'expert judgment'? Kaplan, whom I consider the prominent spokesman for the old-timers, and long-time partner of Norman Kay, told me: ''When considering which card to play, I try to put myself in Norman's head and figure out whether or not he needs any information, and if so, what. Accordingly, I play a card which in the given instance may be a count, attitude or suit preference signal. I also look at the problem from declarer's angle and, if necessary, play the card nearest my thumb.''

Well, if that is not expert judgment then what is? Bobby Wolff, who with partner Bob Hamman is another of my 'old-timers', also asks himself whether the card he is contemplating playing will help partner or declarer.

The ultramoderns are represented by a young group of highly successful expert pairs like Meckstroth-Rodwell, Bergen-Cohen, Woolsey-Manfield, Boyd-Robinson and Lipsitz-Silverman, to name but a few. They believe in frequent signals, particularly giving count and suit preference. ''Every card tells a story'' could be their motto. Marty Bergen likes to stress the importance of signaling in 'nothing' suits: those long suits that the opponents are running. If one defender has a selection of low cards, he may convey a message about a crucial side suit with the order in which he plays those low cards, as I described earlier in this chapter. The Smith Echo is a special case of this approach.

Ed Manfield believes that early in the game signals should be honest because the defenders do not yet know enough about the hand.

The bulk of our American experts belong to the group of 'freelancers'. Here we encounter such experienced partnerships as Pender-Ross, Martel-Stansby, Kantar-Eisenberg and Goldman-Soloway, as well stars like Andersen, Lair, Lawrence, Passell and Wold who play with various partners. Mike Passell points out that the defender who can first diagnose the path the defense should take must assume control. Often, he can do as he pleases, false-card or be honest, but his partner must give true signals. Soloway stresses that the defender with a Yarborough should take great care in giving count, whereas his partner may take all the liberties he wishes to try to lead declarer astray.

The following hand is from the 1982 Mexican Nationals.

```
Dlr: South          ♠ 8 7
Vul: None           ♡ 9 6 5 3
                    ◊ 9 5 2
                    ♣ K 9 6 5
    ♠ 5 3 2                        ♠ K Q J 10 9
    ♡ 10 7 4 2                     ♡ Q J 8
    ◊ 8 6 4                        ◊ Q J 10 3
    ♣ 8 4 3                        ♣ 7
                    ♠ A 6 4
                    ♡ A K
                    ◊ A K 7
                    ♣ A Q J 10 2
```

West	North	East	South
Rosenkranz		Wold	
			2 ♣
Pass	2 ◊	2 ♠	3 ♣
Pass	4 ♣	Pass	6 ♣
Pass	Pass	Pass	

I led the two of spades, and declarer ducked Eddie's nine. South won the spade continuation, ruffed his last spade in the dummy and ran all his trumps. On the last round, should East discard a heart or a diamond? Knowing my diamonds could be of no use, I discarded first the four and then the six, showing an odd number. This was all that Wold needed to know; on the last trump he threw a heart and the slam was defeated.

98

I am not too familiar with the signaling habits outside North America. But I do know there is an important British school that believes in showing count all the time, not even giving attitude at trick one. At the other extreme, the Italians all use odd-even signals, giving precedence to attitude, but possibly issuing a suit preference signal with the size of even card played when not liking the suit partner is attacking. They give count only when necessary. And it seems that in areas where match-pointed pair events are frequent — such as France, the Netherlands, Great Britain and Scandinavia — there is a lot more signaling than in countries where IMP scoring is predominant. This is logical because at pairs the extra overtrick or undertrick is all-important, whereas at team play the defenders have to visualize a layout of the cards which can result in the defeat of the contract; overtricks are relatively insignificant.

By now you have probably formed your own conclusions, and maybe you have decided to signal frequently in weak fields and to 'mix it up' against experts. But the most important thing is to discuss the different situations with your partner so that you know what to expect from his signals.

My Tip for a Top

It is not so important how you signal but rather knowing which signal is being given and when.

Chapter 2

Make Your Signals Crystal Clear

I have only one eye, — I have the right to be blind
sometimes: . . . I really do not see the signal!
At the Battle of Copenhagen, *Horatio, Lord Nelson*

Being stingy with high cards and obscure with signals has cost thousands of defenders money, masterpoints, matches and medals. In 1979, watching the eighth match between two undefeated teams at the Mexican National Swiss Team Championship, I witnessed the following deal:

Dlr: West
Vul: None

♠ A K 3		
♡ K J		
◇ A Q 6 2		
♣ J 9 5 3		

	♠ 9 5 2
	♡ 2
	◇ K 10 8 5 4
	♣ Q 10 4 2

West	North	East	South
3 ♡	3NT	Pass	4 ♠
Pass	Pass	Pass	

West led the ace of hearts and continued with the seven, which East ruffed with the five of spades as South contributed the eight and nine. What would you lead now?

At the time East was reluctant to lead away from his king of diamonds into dummy's tenace, and so returned the two of clubs. South won, drew trumps in two rounds and gave up a diamond trick to make his contract.

At the other table, though, West intelligently led the *queen* of hearts at trick two. This unusual and unnecessary waste of an honor card would have alerted even the most sleepy partner that he was making a suit preference signal asking for the return of the higher of the other two suits: namely, diamonds. Obediently East returned the eight of diamonds at trick three, into the jaws of dummy's ace-queen, and West ruffed. As East still had to win a trick with the king of diamonds, the contract was defeated, the match won and the championship annexed.

This was the complete deal:

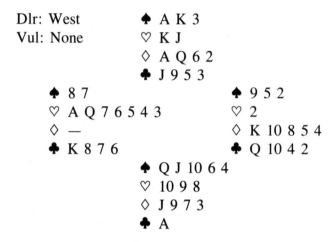

Dlr: West
Vul: None

♠ A K 3
♡ K J
♢ A Q 6 2
♣ J 9 5 3

♠ 8 7
♡ A Q 7 6 5 4 3
♢ —
♣ K 8 7 6

♠ 9 5 2
♡ 2
♢ K 10 8 5 4
♣ Q 10 4 2

♠ Q J 10 6 4
♡ 10 9 8
♢ J 9 7 3
♣ A

The following hand is taken from Eddie Kantar's excellent book, *Defensive Bridge Play Complete*.

Dlr: West
Vul: None

♠ J 7 6
♡ K Q 8
♢ 7 6 5
♣ 8 7 3 2

♠ 5 4
♡ J 10 2
♢ A 10 9 2
♣ J 9 6 4

West	North	East	South
West	*North*	*East*	*South*
1 ♡	Pass	2 ♡	4 ♠
Pass	Pass	Pass	

Partner leads the ace of hearts; which card do you play?

It is clear (and will be to partner as well) that a heart continuation can serve no purpose, so you should make a suit preference signal, dropping the jack (the highest card you have) in order to suggest a diamond switch.

This was the full deal:

Dlr: West
Vul: None

♠ J 7 6
♡ K Q 8
♢ 7 6 5
♣ 8 7 3 2

♠ Q
♡ A 9 7 6 5 3
♢ K J 3
♣ Q 10 5

♠ 5 4
♡ J 10 2
♢ A 10 9 2
♣ J 9 6 4

♠ A K 10 9 8 3 2
♡ 4
♢ Q 8 4
♣ A K

At trick two, West switches to the three of diamonds, East wins with the ace and returns the suit to collect three diamond tricks and defeat the contract.

The final deal in this chapter is more difficult.

Dlr: South   ♠ K J 5
Vul: Both   ♡ Q J 8 7
                ◊ K Q 5
                ♣ K Q 6
                        ♠ 2
                        ♡ 9 6 3
                        ◊ 10 9 8 3
                        ♣ J 9 7 5 4

West	North	East	South
			2 ◊ (a)
Pass	2NT (b)	Pass	3 ♡ (c)
Pass	4 ♡	Pass	Pass
Pass			

(a) Flannery: a minimum opener with four spades and five hearts
(b) What is your shape?   (c) 4-5-2-2 and 12-13 points

Partner, genius that he is, leads the ace of spades, five, two and six. He continues with the seven of spades, dummy plays the king, you ruff with the six of hearts and declarer drops the eight. What do you return now?

Obviously, to beat this hand you must get partner on lead and receive another spade ruff. But why didn't he make his suit preference signal clearer? He must have a higher and a lower spade in his hand with which to tell you where he has his entry. How annoying!

But instead of grinding your teeth, consider that there may be method in partner's apparent madness. Presumably he has neither minor-suit ace. And as declarer must have the queen of spades (partner would not lead the suit from ace-queen-fifth), there is only one chance: lead a *trump!*

This was the full deal:

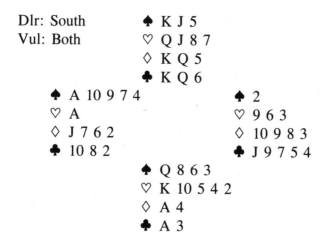

Dlr: South
Vul: Both

```
              ♠ K J 5
              ♡ Q J 8 7
              ◊ K Q 5
              ♣ K Q 6
♠ A 10 9 7 4              ♠ 2
♡ A                      ♡ 9 6 3
◊ J 7 6 2                ◊ 10 9 8 3
♣ 10 8 2                 ♣ J 9 7 5 4
              ♠ Q 8 6 3
              ♡ K 10 5 4 2
              ◊ A 4
              ♣ A 3
```

If you return a minor, declarer can make the contract by discarding both his remaining spades before touching trumps. But when you play a heart to partner's ace, he gives you the fatal second ruff. (Do not ask me why North did not prefer three notrump!)

My Tip for a Top

Be clear with your suit preference (and other) signals. Play the highest or lowest card you can afford; do not dilly-dally with obscure middling cards if you know which suit you want to be returned — unless either you have no preference or need a trump return.

Chapter 3

Suit Preference Signals in the Trump Suit

How can I tell the signals and the signs
By which one heart another heart divines?
Emma and Eginhard, *Henry Wadsworth Longfellow*

Signals are in fashion, the *dernier cri* nowadays. Roman discards, upside-down count and attitude, Vinje signals, revolving, Lavinthal, and so on; seemingly a never-ending list. They are all designed to try to help defenders counter the considerable advantage enjoyed by the declarer.

Not that I disapprove of signaling; on the contrary, I make my fair share of signals in an effort to obtain the maximum number of tricks when defending. As I explained two chapters ago, in my established partnerships we have a hierarchy of signals: attitude, count, suit preference; as has been accepted by the majority of bridge players. Normally one makes an attitude signal, but if that is known, count is usually given; and occasionally suit preference crops up.

What about in the trump suit? Most players use an echo to show exactly three trumps (and often the desire for a ruff), and play up the line with two or four.

Yet why should we not make use of the trumps for signaling purposes? How often do you hold four unimportant cards in the trump suit? Obviously infrequently, but when you do you know partner must be short. When declarer draws trumps your partner must make discards and might be unsure of which suits to retain and which to abandon. When you can make a signal in another suit, it may be too late. Therefore it seems a good idea to signal in the trump suit to show suit preference. You will probably be surprised how this simple signal may save the day for your side and bolster partnership confidence.

Here is how it works: Let us assume that you hold four low trumps: 7 6 4 2. You give count on the first round by playing the two. At your next turn you have three left and may play them in these orders: 4 6 7, 4 7 6, 6 4 7, 6 7 4, 7 4 6 or 7 6 4. It is recommended for serious partnerships to assign meanings to each of these possibilities; though you will probably find that you do not need them all.

One treatment is to play down the line (7 6 4) to show interest in the highest-ranking suit; up the line (4 6 7) as a preference for the lowest-ranking suit; and a MUD sequence (6 7 4) to point toward the middle-ranking suit (in all three cases ignoring the trump suit, of course). Any other order could convey the message of no particular interest.

This method of signaling came in handy during the 1985 Life Master Pairs in Las Vegas.

```
Dlr: South        ♠ 6 5 4 2
Vul: Both         ♡ A Q 10 2
                  ◊ A 6 3
                  ♣ A 6
    ♠ K 9 7 3                    ♠ A J 10 8
    ♡ —                          ♡ J 6 5 4
    ◊ J 9 7 4                    ◊ 10 2
    ♣ J 9 7 3 2                  ♣ Q 10 8
                  ♠ Q
                  ♡ K 9 8 7 3
                  ◊ K Q 8 5
                  ♣ K 5 4
```

West	North	East	South
			1 ♡
Pass	3 ♡ (a)	Pass	4 ♡
Pass	Pass	Pass	

(a) Forcing, of course!

106

My partner, Eddie Wold, led the two of clubs (we use third-and-fifth highest against suit contracts), I played the queen and declarer won with the king. The three of hearts was led to the dummy and Wold had the easy discard of a club, whilst I gave count with the four. On the next lead of the ace of hearts from the dummy, I could afford to part with the jack! This play indicated interest in the highest-ranking suit, spades. Now Wold had no problem as he could discard spades and hold on to the minors.

Notice that without this suit preference signal a club discard could have been wrong, and a diamond would have been fatal, giving declarer twelve tricks: five trumps, four diamonds, two clubs and a club ruff. Holding South to eleven tricks gave us over average.

Of course, Wold would probably have made the right discards anyway, but why not help partner and avoid giving him a chance to go wrong?

The next example occurred in the same event.

```
Dlr: North        ♠ —
Vul: Both         ♡ A J 9 8 5
                  ◇ Q
                  ♣ Q 10 8 7 6 3 2
     ♠ Q 6                      ♠ 9 4 3 2
     ♡ Q 10 6 2                 ♡ K 7 4 3
     ◇ J 10 8 7                 ◇ K 9 4 3
     ♣ K 5 4                    ♣ A
                  ♠ A K J 10 8 7 5
                  ♡ —
                  ◇ A 6 5 2
                  ♣ J 9
```

West	North	East	South
	Pass	Pass	4 ♠
Pass	Pass	Pass	

West, Joey Silver, led the jack of diamonds, queen, king and ace. Declarer started to run the spades, being pleased to see the queen tumble. On the third round Silver threw a club and his partner, Allan Graves, thoughtfully dropped the nine. That did not mean anything until Silver saw the four on the next round, but then he knew he could afford to discard hearts. They held the declarer to his eight top tricks, taking two clubs and three diamonds.

In our methods, we would have thrown the nine on the *second* round to indicate hearts, it being most unlikely that declarer had begun with only ♠ A K 10 8 7 5.

My Tip for a Top

With four worthless trumps, help partner with his discarding problems by signaling your suit preference on the second round of the suit. Play your remaining trumps in ascending order to indicate preference for the lowest-ranking suit, or in descending order for the highest-ranking.

Chapter 4

Preventing the Interior Block
of a Long Suit

To see and be seen, in heaps they run;
Some to undo, and some to be undone.
Trans. of Ovid, Art of Love, *John Dryden*

One of the most frustrating defensive problems — for intermediate players and experts alike — is to run an established suit against a notrump contract without blocking it.

During the 1984 Spring Nationals I witnessed two national title-holders grapple unsuccessfully with this problem during the Men's Board-a-Match teams.

```
Dlr: South        ♠ Q 10 7 6 2
Vul: E-W          ♡ 10 8 2
                  ◇ 7
                  ♣ Q 8 6 2
   ♠ K J 9 8 3               ♠ 5
   ♡ J 6                     ♡ Q 9 7 4
   ◇ 10 6 4 2                ◇ A Q J 9 8
   ♣ 10 9                    ♣ J 7 5
                  ♠ A 4
                  ♡ A K 5 3
                  ◇ K 5 3
                  ♣ A K 4 3
```

South played in three notrump, and West led the two of diamonds, dummy contributed the seven and East, happy that his partner was clairvoyant, put in the jack. Declarer won with the king and played the ace and another spade to West's king. He continued accurately with the four of diamonds, but now put yourself in East's place. Of course, if by agreement partner does not lead low from three or four cards without an honor, you have no problem: you win the trick with the eight and cash the suit. But this arrangement is not universal and did not exist with the expert partnership in question. So East won with the queen and cashed the ace. Who can blame West for failing to throw his ten of diamonds under the ace? But now the suit was blocked and nine tricks were made, winning the board.

Somewhat irritated, East, who is a good friend of mine, turned to me and asked: "Do you have a solution to this problem?"

"Yes," I replied. "To alert partner that you need him to do something unusual, you play your winners in an unusual order, winning the second round of the suit with the ace and then continuing with the queen. This strange sequence of plays asks him to do something unexpected; here, to unblock the ten."

The situation would be the same if the suit were distributed thus:

North
◊ 7

West   *East*
◊ 9 6 4 2   ◊ A Q J 8 5

South
◊ K 10 3

Assuming West leads the two or six, East plays the jack on the first round, the ace on the second and the queen on the third to ask for the unblock.

My Tip for a Top

Alert partner to the need for an unblock by playing your equal cards in an unusual order: the highest followed by the next-highest, rather than in the more natural ascending sequence.

Chapter 5

More on Unblocking

Now mark me how I will undo myself.
Richard III, *William Shakespeare*

In the last chapter I started to consider unblocking plays, and
included in this theme are also deals in which one player must
overtake his partner's card.

You hold ace-third in a suit and your left-hand opponent is
playing in a notrump contract. Your partner surprises you
agreeably by leading the king of this suit, and you signal for
a continuation. Partner follows up with the queen; should you
overtake or not? Obviously if partner has led from a three-card
holding, there is no desire to set up tricks for the opposition.
However, if partner started with K Q J x (x), you should be
overtaking so that the suit does not become blocked.

Similar situations occur when partner's sequence is Q J 10
or J 10 9 rather than Q J 10 x (x) or J 10 9 x (x).

My recommendation for avoiding being faced with a dilem-
ma in this sort is to play the three-card sequences in descending order; whereas with four or more cards to lead the highest
and follow with the lowest of the touching honors.

That gives these possibilities

Sequence Held	Card Led	Second Card Played
K Q J	K	Q
K Q J x (x)	K	J
Q J 10	Q	J
Q J 10 x (x)	Q	10

Here is an example deal from the 1984 Vanderbilt.

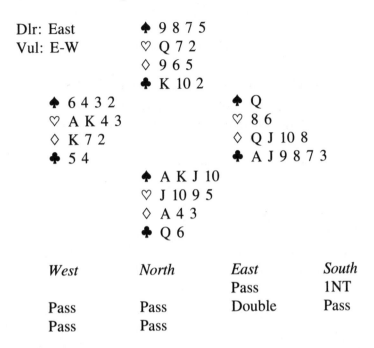

Dlr: East
Vul: E-W

```
                    ♠ 9 8 7 5
                    ♡ Q 7 2
                    ◇ 9 6 5
                    ♣ K 10 2
    ♠ 6 4 3 2                      ♠ Q
    ♡ A K 4 3                      ♡ 8 6
    ◇ K 7 2                        ◇ Q J 10 8
    ♣ 5 4                          ♣ A J 9 8 7 3
                    ♠ A K J 10
                    ♡ J 10 9 5
                    ◇ A 4 3
                    ♣ Q 6
```

West	North	East	South
		Pass	1NT
Pass	Pass	Double	Pass
Pass	Pass		

My partner, Eddie Wold, doubled to show a long club suit as a bid of two clubs would have been Landy, promising a major two-suiter. With no attractive bid, I decided to gamble on defending.

I led the five of clubs, dummy's ten was put in, Wold covered with the jack and declarer correctly ducked. Wold, knowing that he did not have an entry if he established his clubs, now switched to the queen of diamonds. When South ducked, Wold continued with the *ten* of diamonds to indicate at least four cards headed by the queen-jack-ten. If he had had only three diamonds, Wold would have continued with the jack, not the ten.

Declarer won the second diamond with the ace, so I unblocked the king. A heart was taken with my king, and in case partner had started with ace-queen-jack-sixth of clubs, I returned to that suit. However, we were able to take two hearts, three diamonds and two clubs to defeat the contract by one trick.

At the other table the opening one-notrump bid was passed out and the contract made exactly after a heart lead by West; so we gained seven IMPs.

Are you thinking that my unblock of the king of diamonds was unnecessary? This is not so if declarer plays the queen of clubs immediately, knocking out Wold's entry to the long diamond.

My Tip for a Top

To indicate the length of a sequence containing three touching honors, play in descending order with exactly the three honors, but play the highest followed by the lowest of the touching honors when holding four or more cards in the suit.

Chapter 6

Even More Unblocking Problems

Does the silk-worm expend her yellow labours
For thee? for thee does she undo herself?
The Revenger's Tragedy, *Cyril Tourneur*

Another frequent cause of annoyance for defenders is the following: Partner gets off to the best lead against a notrump contract and you hold five cards in the suit. You make your natural play and declarer wins the first trick. Some time later you gain the lead and return your original fourth best. Not knowing about your length, partner wins the trick cheaply and blocks the suit.

For example, the layout might be:

	Dummy ♡ 10	
Partner ♡ A J 8 3		You ♡ Q 9 7 4 2
	Declarer ♡ K 6 5	

Partner leads the three and your queen is captured by declarer's king. When you get on lead you return the four and partner wins the second trick with the eight instead of the jack. How can you avoid this problem?

The standard expert practice nowadays is to give partner the 'residual' or 'present' count when returning the suit. Thus you can build up a table:

Original Holding	Card Returned
K 5	5
K 9 4	9
K 9 4 2	2
K 9 8 4 2	4
K 9 7 4 2	4

In the last case you have four cards remaining, so should echo, but it is also traditional to return your original fourth best. However, how does partner know that you started with a five-card suit rather than with K 9 7 4 and that declarer is hiding the two? Often he will be able to work out the position, particularly if declarer won the first trick with the ace rather than making a hold-up play, but it is more comfortable to have a rule to cover these situations.

We play that with four cards remaining in a suit partner has led where he is marked with length, we return the *highest card we can afford.* If the top two cards are touching, we return the highest; otherwise we play back our second highest.

Using the examples given above, we modify the table to give these plays:

Original Holding	Card Returned
K 5	5
K 9 4	9
K 9 4 2	2
K 9 8 4 2	9
K 9 7 4 2	7

There appears to be ambiguity concerning the return of the nine, but partner should have no trouble working out whether you hold three cards or five in the suit from the bidding and play.

Here is a good example from the Swiss teams at the 1984 Mexican Nationals.

```
Dlr: South          ♠ A J 10 5 2
Vul: Both           ♡ J
                    ◇ K J 10
                    ♣ J 8 6 4
       ♠ 9                        ♠ K 8 7 6 4
       ♡ A 10 8 2                 ♡ Q 9 7 4 3
       ◇ 9 8 6 3                  ◇ 5 2
       ♣ Q 9 7 5                  ♣ 10
                    ♠ Q 3
                    ♡ K 6 5
                    ◇ A Q 7 4
                    ♣ A K 3 2
```

West	North	East	South
			1 ◇
Pass	1 ♠	Pass	2NT
Pass	3NT	Pass	Pass
Pass			

My partner, Eddie Wold, led the two of hearts and declarer won my queen with his king. South immediately tried the spade finesse, but I won with the king. Left with ♡ 9 7 4 3, I returned the *seven*. When declarer played the five Wold could have won the trick cheaply with the eight and blocked the suit, as happened at the other table when East returned the four, his original fourth best. But Wold knew from the bidding that South could not have five hearts, so he won the trick with the ten, cashed the ace and returned the eight so that I could take two more tricks to defeat the contract.

My Tip for a Top

When partner leads a suit against a notrump contract in which you hold five cards, avoid any ambiguity and a potential blockage by returning the top card if the two highest are touching or your second highest if they are not. Only return your fourth best when you started with exactly four cards in the suit.

Chapter 7

Wait for the Light!

*Whose high endeavours are an inward light
That makes the path before him always bright:
Who, with a natural instinct to discern
What knowledge can perform, is diligent to learn.*
Character of the Happy Warrior, *William Wordsworth*

One of our best young players in Mexico City came up to me with a tale of woe: he had lost first place in the Open Pairs at a large Californian Regional by misdefending the following hand.

```
Dlr: North      ♠ J 5
Vul: None       ♡ J 4
                ◊ K J 4
                ♣ Q J 10 9 8 6
    ♠ 9 6 3
    ♡ 9 6 2
    ◊ 10 9 8 3
    ♣ K 5 3
```

West	North	East	South
	3♣	Pass	4NT (a)
Pass	5♣ (b)	Pass	6NT
Pass	Pass	Pass	

(a) Roman Key Card Blackwood   (b) 0 or 3 key cards

My friend had made the reasonable selection of the ten of diamonds for his opening lead, dummy had held the first trick and the queen of clubs had been run to his king.

"What do you lead back?" he asked.

"Hold it," I said. "First I want to know a few things. Who is your partner?"

"One of the leading ten in the Top 500."

"What were your partner's and declarer's cards at trick one?"

"The five from partner and the two from South."

"Then I lead back a heart," was my answer.

An expression of chagrin crossed his face. "Why on earth did you choose a heart over a spade?"

It transpired that the spade switch had let declarer make his contract as this was the full deal:

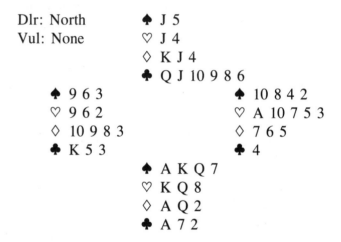

```
Dlr: North        ♠ J 5
Vul: None         ♡ J 4
                  ◇ K J 4
                  ♣ Q J 10 9 8 6
   ♠ 9 6 3                    ♠ 10 8 4 2
   ♡ 9 6 2                    ♡ A 10 7 5 3
   ◇ 10 9 8 3                 ◇ 7 6 5
   ♣ K 5 3                    ♣ 4
                  ♠ A K Q 7
                  ♡ K Q 8
                  ◇ A Q 2
                  ♣ A 7 2
```

I suggested that an expert partner would try to help indicate the winning defense. As it was likely partner had a major-suit ace, he would give a suit preference signal at trick one. As he played a low diamond, I felt he would have the ace of hearts, not the ace of spades. With the latter card, he would have contributed his highest diamond spot at trick one.

I asked my friend what his partner had said at the time. He replied: "Exactly what you did!"

That is rather high-level, so I had another suggestion for my friend: often it could be right to duck the king of clubs at trick two. Declarer must play another club and partner can give a clear signal.

However, that ploy would not be without risk if the contract were six clubs, not six notrump. And on this hand it would be fatal. When declarer sees East discard on the second round of clubs, he puts up the ace and runs four spade winners, discarding dummy's heart losers. West ruffs the fourth round, but it is too late.

A similar example occurred during the semifinal of the Vanderbilt a few years ago. This was the position:

```
Dlr: North        ♠ 7 3
Vul: Both         ♡ 10 7 5
                  ◇ K 9 8 7 6 4 3
                  ♣ 3
     ♠ J 9 6
     ♡ 9 8 3
     ◇ A Q 5
     ♣ Q J 8 6
```

West	North	East	South
Goldman	Roth	Soloway	Tomchin
	2NT (a)	Pass	3 ◇ (b)
Pass	4 ◇	Pass	5 ◇
Pass	Pass	Pass	

(a) Three-bid in a minor   (b) Forcing, asking for the suit

Bobby Goldman led the queen of clubs, partner put in the four and declarer won with the ace. Next came the jack of diamonds, Goldman ducked and dummy won with the king, Soloway dropping the two. On the next round of trumps, East played the ten, South discarded the six of hearts and West won with the queen.

How would you plan the defense from here?

You need to find partner with a trick in one of the majors, but if you pick the wrong one and declarer is very strong in the other, he might be able to discard all of dummy's losers. Goldman solved the problem by cashing the ace of diamonds. Soloway signaled violently in spades, and a switch to that suit defeated the contract.

This was the full deal:

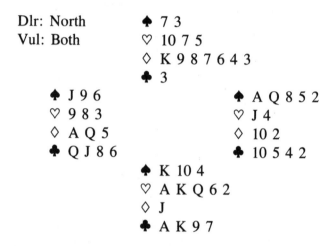

Dlr: North
Vul: Both

```
               ♠ 7 3
               ♡ 10 7 5
               ◊ K 9 8 7 6 4 3
               ♣ 3
 ♠ J 9 6                        ♠ A Q 8 5 2
 ♡ 9 8 3                        ♡ J 4
 ◊ A Q 5                        ◊ 10 2
 ♣ Q J 8 6                      ♣ 10 5 4 2
               ♠ K 10 4
               ♡ A K Q 6 2
               ◊ J
               ♣ A K 9 7
```

Note that a heart switch lets the game through. Declarer wins in hand, discards one of dummy's spades on the king of clubs and then runs three more rounds of hearts, dummy's last spade disappearing while West harmlessly ruffs in. Also, if declarer's majors are switched round, it would be imperative to play a heart.

My Tip for a Top

If, during the defense of a contract, you are not sure how to continue, try to wait for the guiding light from partner. Whenever it is safe, postpone the winning or cashing of a trick until partner is able to give the revealing signal.

Chapter 8

The Rule of Fourteen

Quatorze? Le bon Dieu n'a que dix.

Fourteen? The good Lord has only ten.
Georges Clemenceau
(Attributed after hearing of Woodrow Wilson's Fourteen Points)

The chances are that you do not use the 'Rule of Fourteen'; the likelihood is that you have never heard of it. Neither have the experts. The fact is that I named it myself shortly before writing this exposé.

At the table experts use it without thinking about it in such simple terms. Yet it is so logical and simple that you can follow their defensive reasoning with a fundamental piece of arithmetic. Whenever the opponents reach three notrump after a quantitative auction, you are able to assume that they have about 26 high-card points between their two hands. For example, the bidding might go as in the following two auctions:

	West	North	East	South
a.				1NT
	Pass	2♣	Pass	2◊ / ♡ / ♠
	Pass	2NT	Pass	3NT
	Pass	Pass	Pass	
b.		1◊	Pass	1NT
	Pass	2NT	Pass	3NT
	Pass	Pass	Pass	

If the opponents have 26 points between them, you and your partner must have the remaining fourteen. So if you subtract your total from fourteen, you have the number partner must be holding (within one point either way).

In general, you may use this as a guide to whether you should try to establish the setting tricks in partner's hand or your own. Often this will lead you to the winning defense — if there is one.

Here are two remarkable examples of this thought process in action. You are sitting West, holding

♠ 10 9 8 3   ♡ A 10 3   ◇ K J 4   ♣ Q 8 2

and you hear the auction proceed:

West	North	East	South
			1NT (a)
Pass	2♣	Pass	2◇
Pass	2NT	Pass	3NT
Pass	Pass	Pass	

(a) 15-17 points

What is your opening lead?

You have ten high-card points, so your partner rates to have about four. As a consequence, there is not a lot of point in try- ing to find a good, strong suit in partner's hand. As declarer is short in the majors, you should make your natural lead of the ten of spades.

This is what you can see:

Dlr: South   ♠ K 5 2
Vul: None   ♡ Q 8 6 5
                 ◇ 9 5
                 ♣ K J 4 3

        ♠ 10 9 8 3
        ♡ A 10 3
        ◇ K J 4
        ♣ Q 8 2

Dummy puts up the king of spades, partner contributes the seven and declarer drops the jack. Next declarer runs dummy's nine of diamonds round to your jack, partner playing the two. What do you lead now?

It looks safe to lead another spade, proposing to continue with a third round when you get in with the king of diamonds. Then, when you regain the lead once more with the ace of hearts, you can cash your fourth spade. However, before doing the obvious without real thought, give the matter some extra consideration.

Trick one told you the whole spade story: declarer must have ♠ A Q J for with ♠ A J x he would have let the lead run round to his hand. Similarly, South presumably has the ace-queen of diamonds for his play at trick two. That accounts for thirteen of his seventeen (or maybe sixteen) points, leaving him with only an ace (or king) unaccounted for. If you play another spade now, if declarer has five diamonds, as seems likely from partner's two, he will make three spade tricks, three diamonds and three clubs with the aid of the winning finesse if he has that ace. Admittedly, if he has the king of hearts and not the ace of clubs, you are going to defeat the contract, but you should always consider partner's plays. Why did he play the seven of spades at trick one even though you know he has three? He must be trying to make an unusual suit preference signal indicating a good heart holding. And if he has king-jack-fourth of hearts, you need to switch to the *ten* of hearts.

This was the full deal:

Dlr: South
Vul: None

	♠ K 5 2	
	♡ Q 8 6 5	
	◇ 9 5	
	♣ K J 4 3	
♠ 10 9 8 3		♠ 7 6 4
♡ A 10 3		♡ K J 7 4
◇ K J 4		◇ 7 6 2
♣ Q 8 2		♣ 10 6 5
	♠ A Q J	
	♡ 9 2	
	◇ A Q 10 8 3	
	♣ A 9 7	

If you switch to the ace of hearts and then the ten, you can defeat the contract as long as partner refrains from cashing the jack of hearts, but expecting you to hold a doubleton he might well feel that if he does not take it then, he never will. And if he does take the jack, declarer can make the contract by way of three spades, one heart, one diamond and four clubs.

You avoid all these problems by switching to the ten of hearts. Dummy covers with the queen, your partner wins with the king and returns a low heart to your ace. Now a third round leaves partner with the jack-seven sitting over dummy's eight-six and the contract is definitely dead. And to put the frosting on the cake, you might even score the king of diamonds for a two-trick defeat.

For the second example, you are still West, looking at

♠ Q 10 9   ♡ Q 10 9 5   ◊ K 7 6   ♣ A Q 10

The bidding goes:

West	North	East	South
			1NT (a)
Pass	2NT	Pass	3NT
Double!	Pass	Pass	Pass

(a) 16-18 points

You might not have doubled, but you still have to lead! What is your choice?

The hand was held by Dick Frey, playing in the 1942 Goldman Pairs in New York, which he won with the late Sonny Moyse. Frey worked out that his partner rated to hold one jack, and the only one that was likely to be any use was the jack of clubs. As a consequence, Frey led the *queen* of clubs!

This was the complete deal:

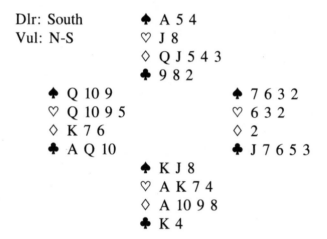

Dlr: South
Vul: N-S

```
                    ♠ A 5 4
                    ♡ J 8
                    ◇ Q J 5 4 3
                    ♣ 9 8 2
  ♠ Q 10 9                         ♠ 7 6 3 2
  ♡ Q 10 9 5                       ♡ 6 3 2
  ◇ K 7 6                          ◇ 2
  ♣ A Q 10                         ♣ J 7 6 5 3
                    ♠ K J 8
                    ♡ A K 7 4
                    ◇ A 10 9 8
                    ♣ K 4
```

Any other start (except the ace of clubs followed by the queen) would have given declarer the time to set up his diamonds and bring home the contract. But the queen-of-clubs lead not only forced out declarer's king, but it also unblocked the suit. Moyse expressed his enthusiasm by dropping the seven, and when Frey got in with the king of diamonds, he continued with the ace and ten of clubs to defeat the contract.

My Tip for a Top

Apply the Rule of Fourteen when the opponents reach three notrump in a limited auction. It will give you a good idea of whether you should lead your long suit or try to find partner's.

Chapter 9

Drawing Inferences

"I should have more faith," he said; "I ought to know by this time than when a fact appears opposed to a long train of deductions, it invariably proves to be capable of bearing some other interpretation."

A Study in Scarlet, *Sir Arthur Conan Doyle*

Great dummy players do not grow on trees; they develop because often they have found themselves in tight spots and have learned through bitter experience how to bring home nearly impossible contracts or to escape astronomical penalties, paying only a modest price. How do they do it?

Apart from practice making perfect, every declarer has a great advantage: he knows his total resources all the time; whereas the defenders can only draw inferences from the bidding and card-play; they are often left in the dark as to the total of their combined assets. The tempo or first strike of the opening lead is, of course, a weapon which goes some way to neutralizing declarer's advantage, but it does not compensate completely. Therefore, it cannot be stressed often enough that to be a successful defender you have to use every clue, every signal, every inference that comes your way.

Counting is the single most important facet of defense, but in this chapter I wish to concentrate on drawing inferences from the play. But thinking does not start there. You should be trying to build up pictures of the other player's hands during the bidding. Next, when the dummy hits the table, consider how that alters the ideas you had. At this point a good declarer will stop to plan his campaign, but if he plays rapidly from the dummy and you are third hand, do not let yourself be bulldozed into a disadvantageous rhythm of play: Tell the declarer you are thinking about the whole hand, not this particular trick. Ask yourself questions like: Is the dummy stronger than you expected? If so, maybe you will only be concerned with saving overtricks. On the other hand, if it is weaker than anticipated, you should have a chance to defeat the contract.

As the play proceeds, try to get into the habit of asking yourself: What is declarer up to? Endeavor to figure out his game plan, and if he does something unusual — a play you did not anticipate — stop to think and strive to work out a reason for this unexpected move. You should attempt to maintain an even tempo of play, but do not be shy; there is nothing wrong with a time out. And, of course, trying to work out what is going on, paradoxical as it may sound, is easier against a competent declarer than against someone who does not know what he is doing.

Learning to draw inferences from declarer's play is the subject of the following quiz on single-suit situations.

1. You hold K x x in front of a dummy rich in entries. Declarer leads a low card toward dummy's J 10 x. What do you know?

2. Against a notrump contract, partner leads the four of a suit, the low card promising an honor. Dummy holds Q 5 and you have K 10 6 3. Declarer plays low from the dummy; what do you infer, and what is your play?

3. The contract is a partscore in a suit. Partner leads the five of a side suit and dummy displays the ace-queen doubleton. You hold 10 8 6 4, and declarer puts up dummy's ace. What is going on in the suit?

4. Your partner leads the four of a suit against three notrump. Dummy comes down with J 10 7, and declarer calls for the seven. You are looking at K 8 3; what do you make of it?

5. You hold K x x behind dummy's A Q x x. A low card is led from the dummy; what do you do?

These are hopefully the answers you came up with:

1. Unless the position of your king is marked by the previous bidding, you should assume that the declarer does not hold A Q x (x) because with sufficient entries to the dummy, he would have tried the finesse. Either your partner has the ace

or declarer has A x x (no nine) and is hoping you will rise with an honor. Do not put up your king.

2. Declarer cannot have the ace because if he did, he would have inserted the queen from the dummy. More likely he has jack-doubleton or jack-third. Go up with the king and lead back the three, your original fourth best. With luck, partner will have started with ace-fifth.

3. As declarer did not finesse, the inference is that he has the king and has possibly made a poor play by not concealing the situation from you by putting in the queen. The other possibility is that he has a singleton; but probably the bidding will tell you whether or not that is likely.

4. Unless you are running the suit, you may assume that declarer has the queen, not the ace. With the latter honor, he would put up dummy's jack — unless, of course, he also has the nine.

5. Once more, information at the declarer's finger tips may influence his play, but otherwise you may assume he could have the jack. Unless you need to cash tricks in a hurry, though, it is probably right to play low. Declarer may have a worthless tripleton.

Finally, an example dealing with a frequent situation.

Dlr: North
Vul: None

♠ K J 2
♡ 6
◇ A Q J 10 8 5 4
♣ J 6

♠ A 5 4 3
♡ 10 5 4
◇ 9 3 2
♣ 10 9 3

West	North	East	South
	1 ◇	Pass	1 ♡
Pass	2 ◇	Pass	3NT
Pass	Pass	Pass	

It is a matchpointed pair event, and you lead the ten of clubs. Dummy plays the six, your partner contributes the two and declarer wins with the king. At trick two declarer leads the six of spades. What do you infer and how do you defend?

Why isn't declarer playing on diamonds? Answer: he must have the king. So he is trying to steal a trick before the defenders can signal to each other. Take your ace; you may not get another chance.

This was the full deal:

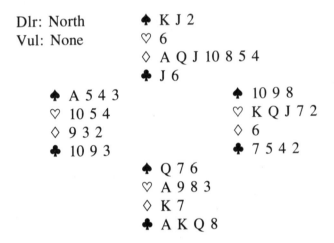

Dlr: North
Vul: None

♠ K J 2
♡ 6
◊ A Q J 10 8 5 4
♣ J 6

♠ A 5 4 3
♡ 10 5 4
◊ 9 3 2
♣ 10 9 3

♠ 10 9 8
♡ K Q J 7 2
◊ 6
♣ 7 5 4 2

♠ Q 7 6
♡ A 9 8 3
◊ K 7
♣ A K Q 8

Of course, the less said about the bidding the better with a cold slam in diamonds missed. However, if you ducked your ace of spades, hoping declarer would misguess, he will have made thirteen tricks and salvaged some matchpoints.

My Tip for a Top

When defending, don't just follow suit mechanically; attempt to build up a mental picture of how the cards are distributed around the table, and try to figure out declarer's likely plan. Become accustomed to drawing inferences!

Chapter 10

What is Declarer Up To?

This is the sort of English up with which I will not put.
Sir Winston Churchill

In the last chapter we focused on inferences in one-suit situations. Now it is time to move on to more unusual moves by the declarer.

The following important and instructive position arose during the qualifying round of the 1986 Mexican Grand Nationals.

Sitting West, you hold

♠ J 8 4   ♡ 5 2   ◇ 10 8 5 3   ♣ K Q 10 4

The bidding proceeds:

West	North	East	South
			2 ♣
Pass	2 ◇	Pass	2 ♡
Pass	3 ♡	Pass	6 ♡
Pass	Pass	Pass	

You lead the obvious king of clubs, and this is what you can see:

Dlr: South ♠ 9 5 2
Vul: Both   ♡ Q 10 9 4
            ◇ 9 7 4 2
            ♣ 5 3

♠ J 8 4
♡ 5 2
◇ 10 8 5 3
♣ K Q 10 4

Partner plays the nine of clubs and declarer contributes the seven. You continue with the queen of clubs, partner completes an echo with the two and declarer wins with the ace. Next, declarer ruffs the eight of clubs with dummy's ten of hearts, partner dropping the six, and proceeds to draw trumps in two rounds, playing the queen and nine from the table and the three and king from his hand. To your surprise, declarer continues with the ace of hearts from hand. Before making your first discard, ask yourself this question: What is declarer's plan?

Obviously South does not have the jack of clubs. Also, he has enough trump entries, yet he did not take a finesse in either spades or diamonds. So it seems that he must have either ace-king-fourth of spades and a bare ace of diamonds, or both ace-kings and a thirteenth spot-card in one of those suits; but which one? Partner is going to have to decide whether to hold diamonds or spades. You both have a club to pitch now, but what is coming up?

The best play is to discard a small spade immediately. This will tell partner that you do not propose to protect spades and simultaneously give him the count in the suit. Then throw your last club, followed by the eight of spades. With your help, partner will guard the spades, discarding in order his last club, a spade and a diamond.

This was the full deal:

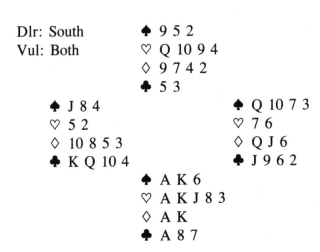

```
Dlr: South        ♠ 9 5 2
Vul: Both         ♡ Q 10 9 4
                  ◇ 9 7 4 2
                  ♣ 5 3
      ♠ J 8 4                    ♠ Q 10 7 3
      ♡ 5 2                      ♡ 7 6
      ◇ 10 8 5 3                 ◇ Q J 6
      ♣ K Q 10 4                 ♣ J 9 6 2
                  ♠ A K 6
                  ♡ A K J 8 3
                  ◇ A K
                  ♣ A 8 7
```

133

At the time, though, the declarer, Sol Dubson, made the contract. West's first discard was his club, and on the next heart he threw the three of diamonds, reasoning that partner had to have an easy spade pitch. On the last heart West finally dumped the four of spades, but the damage had been done and East parted with the seven of spades, allowing the declarer's six of spades to become the twelfth trick. It is true that East might have still got it right because his partner would have thrown the eight of spades from ♠ J 8 6 4, but West made it difficult for his partner.

Notice that the defense against such small slams falls into two categories:

1. The defense has already won a trick. A defender should signal by making his first discard from the suit he is *not* going to hold, giving the count at the same time if possible. If in doubt about which suit to hold, then he should part with an idle card first.

2. If the defenders have not taken a trick, signals should show attitude, indicating a possible source of tricks.

Timeo Danaos et dona ferentis (I fear the Greeks even when they bring gifts) is the motto of the next two hands.

When a competent declarer presents you with an unexpected trick, distrust him and think whether you should accept it.

Dlr: South
Vul: Both

    ♠ 8 4
    ♡ A K J 5 4
    ♢ 6 3 2
    ♣ 7 6 5

♠ J 6
♡ Q 8 6 3
♢ K J 5
♣ 10 9 4 2

West	North	East	South
			2 ♣
Pass	2 ♡ (a)	Pass	2 ♠
Pass	2NT	Pass	3 ♠
Pass	4 ♠	Pass	6 ♠
Pass	Pass	Pass	

(a) A good suit with at least two of the top three honors

You lead the ten of clubs, partner plays the eight, probably indicating an even number of cards, and declarer wins with the king. At trick two declarer leads the ten of spades! How do you defend?

Having heard the warning bell rung during the introduction, no doubt you have ducked, but would have done so at the table? If you won with the jack, you let the contract make as the full deal was:

Dlr: South
Vul: Both

```
              ♠ 8 4
              ♡ A K J 5 4
              ◇ 6 3 2
              ♣ 7 6 5
♠ J 6                        ♠ 5 3 2
♡ Q 8 6 3                    ♡ 10 9 7 2
◇ K J 5                      ◇ 10 9 8 7
♣ 10 9 4 2                   ♣ 8 3
              ♠ A K Q 10 9 7
              ♡ —
              ◇ A Q 4
              ♣ A K Q J
```

Winning with the jack allows declarer to get into the dummy with the eight of spades and his two diamond losers can be parked on the ace and king of hearts. If you pass the test and allow the ten of spades to hold, after ten tricks this will be the position:

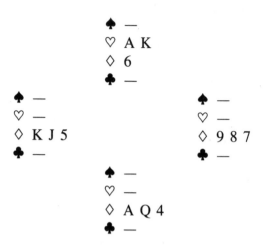

```
        ♠ —
        ♡ A K
        ◊ 6
        ♣ —
♠ —                    ♠ —
♡ —                    ♡ —
◊ K J 5                ◊ 9 8 7
♣ —                    ♣ —
        ♠ —
        ♡ —
        ◊ A Q 4
        ♣ —
```

When declarer leads the four of diamonds, East wins with the seven and returns the suit to ensure a well-deserved 100-point penalty.

Before a weekly duplicate, one of our best up-and-coming players approached me with this problem:

Dlr: South   ♠ A 6
Vul: N-S   ♡ 8 5 2
                   ◊ J 5 4
                   ♣ A 6 4 3 2
    ♠ K 9 8 5 2
    ♡ J 6 3
    ◊ 10 8
    ♣ J 7 5

West	North	East	South
			1♣ (a)
Pass	2♣ (b)	Pass	2NT
Pass	3NT	Pass	Pass
Pass			

(a) Precision   (b) Positive response with at least five clubs

He asked me what I would lead, and I selected the five of spades.

He told me that partner wins the trick with the queen, declarer dropping the four, and that the second trick goes seven of spades, ten, two and ace. A low club from the dummy is covered by East's nine, declarer's king and your five. South now leads the jack of spades, which you win with the king as dummy parts with a heart and partner follows with the three of spades. What do you do now?

After giving it a little thought, I told him that I would switch immediately to the three of hearts. An expression of surprise and disappointment crossed my young friend's face.

"You don't cash your spades?"

"No. Declarer must have a reason for being so generous. Perhaps he is trying for an endplay, an unblocking play or a suicide squeeze. I decline the Greek gift."

"All right. South wins partner's queen of hearts with the king and leads the ten of clubs. What now?"

"I cover with the jack."

"What? You throw away a trick crashing partner's singleton queen?"

"Don't be silly. The club suit is now blocked. Declarer must win with the ace and he has no reentry to dummy's established clubs. But tell me: Did this hand really occur or did you make it up to test me? I saw a similar situation in the book *Positive Defence* by Reese and Pottage."

An embarrassed smile was his answer.

This was the full deal:

Dlr: South   ♠ A 6
Vul: N-S   ♡ 8 5 2
       ♢ J 5 4
       ♣ A 6 4 3 2

♠ K 9 8 5 2   ♠ Q 7 3
♡ J 6 3   ♡ Q 10 9 4
♢ 10 8   ♢ K Q 7 3 2
♣ J 7 5   ♣ 9

      ♠ J 10 4
      ♡ A K 7
      ♢ A 9 6
      ♣ K Q 10 8

If after winning with the king of spades you play only one more round of spades, declarer jettisons the eight or ten of clubs and comes to nine tricks. Furthermore, if you refuse to cover the ten of clubs with your jack, declarer lets it ride and again makes his contract.

My Tip for a Top

Try to get into the habit of using inferences as it is essential for good card-play. And try to anticipate and understand your opponent's moves, being particularly suspicious of unexpected gifts.

Chapter 11

Making Sure Partner
Does the Right Thing

There is no mistake; there has been no mistake; and there
shall be no mistake.
                        Wellingtoniana, *Duke of Wellington*

One of the reasons why I feel a non-playing captain should be
an expert stems from a practice begun long ago. If a pair
were having trouble, they would persuade a fellow expert
to watch a session and record charges for the mishaps that vic-
timize even the top-ranking partnerships. It was his task to point
out not only the obvious errors but also to apportion the guilt
for mistakes which one player made but his partner might
somehow have prevented.

For example, here is a hand cited by Helen Sobel Smith,
whom many consider the most brilliant woman player ever.
I quote from the chapter entitled 'How to Play with a Man'
in her book called *Bridge for Women*.

```
                    ♠ K Q 3
                    ♡ J 10 4
                    ◇ K 7 6 4
                    ♣ K Q 10
    ♠ 8 6 2                        ♠ 7 5
    ♡ K 9 8 3 2                    ♡ A 7
    ◇ Q J 2                        ◇ A 9 8 5 3
    ♣ 7 6                          ♣ 8 5 4 3
                    ♠ A J 10 9 4
                    ♡ Q 6 5
                    ◇ 10
                    ♣ A J 9 2
```

West	North	East	South
			1 ♠
Pass	2NT	Pass	3 ♣
Pass	3 ♠	Pass	4 ♠
Pass	Pass	Pass	

"West opened a low heart and East won the ace. East, all bright-eyed and bushy-tailed, fired back the seven and awaited a heart ruff. East expected that the ace of diamonds would then supply the setting trick.

"But the defense lost its way. On the second round of hearts, South blandly dropped the queen, and when West won the king he took the eminently reasonable position that South might have no more hearts, in which case it would be essential to shift to a diamond. West therefore returned the queen of diamonds. East headed dummy's king with the ace, but South claimed the rest of the tricks.

"Although it was West who failed to give his partner a heart ruff, he was not to blame. East could have made sure of beating the contract by playing off the ace of diamonds before returning the seven of hearts. Cashing the ace of diamonds would have made it plain to West that there were no more tricks to be garnered from that suit."

What if South were void in diamonds? Not very likely, for West, holding ◊ Q J 10 2, would surely have led the queen of diamonds rather than a heart. Besides, if South had a diamond void, the contract could not be defeated.

The next situation involves helping partner make the right play. It occurred in a Grand National qualifying match in New York.

Dlr: North
Vul: None

♠ 8 7 5 4
♡ K Q 9 8 4
◊ 3
♣ A 7 6

♠ A 2
♡ 10 7 2
◊ J 9 8 7 2
♣ J 10 3

West	North	East	South
	Pass	Pass	1 ♠
Double	2NT (a)	Pass	4 ♠
Pass	Pass	Pass	

(a) High-card raise to three spades

West leads the king of diamonds; which card do you play?

As dummy holds a singleton, it looks as though suit preference signals should be in effect (a high diamond asking for a heart switch, a low diamond requesting a club and a middle card either showing no preference or, more likely, suggesting a diamond continuation). In this case, though, it is so unlikely that a heart switch will be the winning defense that these signals do not apply. So, an encouraging diamond from East at trick one is just saying that he thinks it is wrong for the opener leader to make the obvious switch. Here that would be to clubs, and so West is being warned that unless he can make the switch safely himself (holding both the king and queen), he should not play a club but continue diamonds.

This was the full deal:

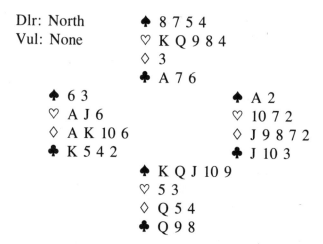

Dlr: North   ♠ 8 7 5 4
Vul: None   ♡ K Q 9 8 4
                 ◊ 3
                 ♣ A 7 6

♠ 6 3   ♠ A 2
♡ A J 6   ♡ 10 7 2
◊ A K 10 6   ◊ J 9 8 7 2
♣ K 5 4 2   ♣ J 10 3

              ♠ K Q J 10 9
              ♡ 5 3
              ◊ Q 5 4
              ♣ Q 9 8

At one table, where East played the nine of diamonds, West continued with the ace of diamonds at trick two. Declarer ruffed in the dummy and led a trump, but East went in immediately with the ace and switched to the jack of clubs, defeating the contract for sure.

At the other table, East dropped the two of diamonds as he did not have the queen. West did the logical-looking thing, switching to a low club. This looked bad, but was in fact not fatal. Declarer won in hand with the queen and played a heart, West keeping his side in the hand by ducking. Declarer won with dummy's king and led a trump, and if East had risen with the ace and played a club, the contract would have still gone down. But vainly hoping that declarer had a guess, East played low, allowing declarer to win with the king and play a second heart. Now the contract was home and the swing was ten IMPs.

What would you do in this position?

Dlr: South   ♠ Q 10 8 5
Vul: Both   ♡ Q J 5 3
              ◊ K J
              ♣ Q 4 2

♠ 4 2
♡ A
◊ Q 9 8 7 6 4
♣ K 7 6 3

West	North	East	South
			1 ♠
Pass	3 ♠	Pass	4 ♠
Pass	Pass	Pass	

You lead your singleton ace of hearts and partner drops a discouraging two. You switch to the three of clubs and partner, fine fellow, wins with the jack and continues with the ace, declarer following with the eight and ten. Things are going well, but is a storm brewing?

143

There is a grave risk that partner will try to cash a third club trick. But you know that this might not stand up, whereas a heart ruff is a certainty to defeat the contract. Open your partner's eyes with a signal on this trick: drop the king of clubs under his ace!

This was the full deal:

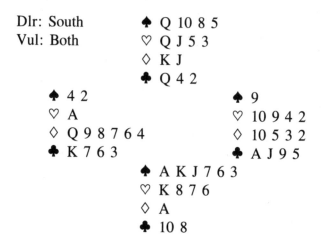

```
Dlr: South          ♠ Q 10 8 5
Vul: Both           ♡ Q J 5 3
                    ◇ K J
                    ♣ Q 4 2
     ♠ 4 2                        ♠ 9
     ♡ A                          ♡ 10 9 4 2
     ◇ Q 9 8 7 6 4                ◇ 10 5 3 2
     ♣ K 7 6 3                    ♣ A J 9 5
                    ♠ A K J 7 6 3
                    ♡ K 8 7 6
                    ◇ A
                    ♣ 10 8
```

This hand would be less of a problem for a pair using third-best leads as when West leads the six at trick two and follows with the three East would know that declarer had started with a doubleton. And as declarer is likely to have the ace of diamonds (or a guaranteed loser in the suit), the heart return is marked; but on another occasion that might not be the case, and dropping the king of clubs is the safe play regardless.

My Tip for a Top

If you are defending and you know how to beat the contract, take charge and stop partner from making an error in the clearest way possible.

Section C
Declarer-Play

The Prelude

Others abide our question. Thou art free.
We ask and ask: Thou smilest and art still,
Out-topping knowledge.

Shakespeare, *Matthew Arnold*

1.
Dlr: East
Vul: None

♠ 7 2
♡ J 9 4
◊ J 9 8 3
♣ J 10 7 4

♠ A 9 6 3
♡ A Q 2
◊ A K Q
♣ A Q 6

West	North	East	South
		1♠	Double
Pass	2♣	Pass	3NT
Pass	Pass	Pass	

West leads the eight of spades and East puts in the ten; plan the play.

(Page 152)

2.

Dlr: West	♠ Q J 5		
Vul: None	♡ A K 9 2		
	◊ 7 4 2		
	♣ A Q 9		

♠ A 6 3 2
♡ J 5
◊ K 10 3
♣ K J 6 3

West	North	East	South
1 ◊	Double	Pass	2 ♠
Pass	3 ◊	Pass	3NT
Pass	Pass	Pass	

West leads the queen of diamonds. What is your line of play?

(Page 155)

3.

Dlr: North	♠ A K 7 6	
Vul: Both	♡ K J 5 2	
	◊ K J	
	♣ K Q J	

♠ 9 4
♡ 10 9 6 3
◊ A Q 5 3
♣ 8 5 3

After a conventional sequence, South has to play in four hearts, and West leads the ten of diamonds. Given that the hand is from a pair event, how would you tackle the play?

(Page 162)

149

4.

Dlr: West   ♠ A 5 2
Vul: E-W   ♡ A K 7
               ◊ K 8 4
               ♣ A 9 6 2

               ♠ K Q 10 8 4 3
               ♡ —
               ◊ Q 5 3
               ♣ K 7 4 3

West	North	East	South
2 ♡	Double	Pass	3 ♡
Pass	3NT	Pass	4 ♠
Pass	6 ♠	Pass	Pass
Pass			

The opening lead is the queen of hearts. How do you plan to bring home twelve tricks?

(Page 167)

5.

               ♠ Q 7 4
               ♡ J 9 7 6 3 2
               ◊ A 8 3
               ♣ A

               ♠ A K J 3 2
               ♡ 8 5
               ◊ K 6 4
               ♣ J 8 3

The contract is four spades and a diamond is led. Plan the play.

(Page 194)

6.

         ♠ Q 7 4
         ♡ J 9 7 6 3 2
         ◇ A 8 3
         ♣ J

         ♠ A K J 3 2
         ♡ 8 5
         ◇ K 6 4
         ♣ A 8 3

Same contract: four spades; and same lead: the ten of diamonds.
Any change in your approach?   (Page 196)

7.
Dlr: West   ♠ 3
Vul: None   ♡ 10 9 8 7 5 4
         ◇ A 10 9 4
         ♣ K 3

         ♠ K J 8 4
         ♡ K
         ◇ K 8 7 6 5
         ♣ A 10 9

West	North	East	South
1 ♡	Pass	Pass	Double
Pass	Pass	1 ♠	Double
2 ♣	Pass	Pass	2 ◇
Pass	3 ◇	Pass	5 ◇
Pass	Pass	Pass	

West cashes the aces of hearts and spades before switching to
the four of clubs. What is your line of play?   (Page 209)

Chapter 1

A Little Knowledge is a Dangerous Thing

If you dissemble sometimes your knowledge of that you are thought to know, you shall be thought, another time, to know that you know not.

Of Discourse, *Francis Bacon*

It is a strange phenomenon of bridge that if you become interested in a certain hypothetical situation, you can be sure that soon you will encounter a typical example at the table.

We all know that hold-up plays are a standard part of every declarer's repertoire, but there are occasions when that technique would be fatal. A part from times when you are more worried about a switch to another suit, this is partciularly true when the bidding has marked one player with all the outstanding high-card strength. In such cases, a hold-up play will be of no help and you are better advised to retain an exit card in the opponent's long suit and attempt a throw-in.

Here is an example.

```
Dlr: East        ♠ 7 2
Vul: None        ♡ J 9 4
                 ◊ J 9 8 3
                 ♣ J 10 7 4
     ♠ 8 4                      ♠ K Q J 10 5
     ♡ 7 6 5 3                  ♡ K 10 8
     ◊ 7 6 4                    ◊ 10 5 2
     ♣ 8 5 3 2                  ♣ K 9
                 ♠ A 9 6 3
                 ♡ A Q 2
                 ◊ A K Q
                 ♣ A Q 6
```

At every table, East opened one spade, and South reached three notrump. Each West led the eight of spades, and most declarers held up their ace for two or three rounds. Then they cashed the diamond winners before playing off the ace and queen of clubs, hoping to force an entry to dummy. As you can see, this was a suicidal play, East winning with the king and cashing enough spade tricks to defeat the contract.

The winning play, with East marked with the three kings, is to take the second or third spade, cash the diamonds and exit with a spade. East is welcome to his tricks, but he is then endplayed to lead away from either of his kings, giving dummy an entry and declarer his contract.

How would you plan the play here?

Dlr: West   ♠ K Q 9 4
Vul: E-W   ♡ K 5 2
                ◇ Q 4
                ♣ K 8 7 4

                ♠ J 10 7
                ♡ A 7 6
                ◇ A 8 6
                ♣ A 9 3 2

West	North	East	South
1 ♡	Pass	Pass	1NT
Pass	3NT	Pass	Pass
Pass			

West leads the queen of hearts and East contributes the nine. What is your line of play?

It is normal, with this heart holding, to duck one round so that if East gains the lead he will not have another heart. However, here you are only missing fourteen high-card points, so that marks West with both the ace of spades and king of diamonds. To make the contract, you will need an endplay, so win the first trick, knock out the ace of spades, win the second heart round and cash your black-suit winners before casting adrift in hearts. West will be able to take some heart tricks (any maybe a club) but will then be forced to lead away from his king of diamonds.

This was the full deal:

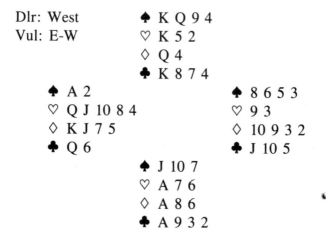

Dlr: West
Vul: E-W

```
                    ♠ K Q 9 4
                    ♡ K 5 2
                    ◊ Q 4
                    ♣ K 8 7 4
  ♠ A 2                          ♠ 8 6 5 3
  ♡ Q J 10 8 4                   ♡ 9 3
  ◊ K J 7 5                      ◊ 10 9 3 2
  ♣ Q 6                          ♣ J 10 5
                    ♠ J 10 7
                    ♡ A 7 6
                    ◊ A 8 6
                    ♣ A 9 3 2
```

Admittedly, West might blank the king of diamonds and defeat you unless you guess correctly, but at least you gave yourself a chance.

My third example deal arose during the 1986 Mexican Grand Nationals.

Dlr: West   ♠ Q J 5
Vul: None   ♡ A K 9 2
             ◊ 7 4 2
             ♣ A Q 9

♠ K 4   ♠ 10 9 8 7
♡ Q 4 3   ♡ 10 8 7 6
◊ A Q J 9 8   ◊ 6 5
♣ 10 4 2   ♣ 8 7 5

         ♠ A 6 3 2
         ♡ J 5
         ◊ K 10 3
         ♣ K J 6 3

West	North	East	South
1 ◊	Double	Pass	2 ♠
Pass	3 ◊	Pass	3NT
Pass	Pass	Pass	

You may not agree with the bidding, but South devalued his
king of diamonds when responding to the take-out double. Then
North checked if his partner had a diamond stopper, and three
notrump was the resultant final contract.

The opening lead was the queen of diamonds and South, a
well-read, solid declarer, held up his king. West, one of our
leading players, immediately recognized the danger of an endplay and continued with the ace and jack of diamonds, East
discarding the ten of spades. South won and cashed his four
club tricks, West throwing a heart, North a spade and East a
spade. Declarer now led the jack of hearts, hoping to find West
down to the queen-ten doubleton. When that failed to
materialize, he finessed in spades and went one down.

This might seem like bad luck, but it is not. The bidding
has marked West with all the outstanding twelve high-card
points. As a consequence, declarer should win the first trick
and cash his four club winners. When West discards a heart,
the ace and king are played in case the queen and ten are drop-

ping. When they do not, West is thrown in with a diamond. He may take four diamond tricks, but then must lead away from his marked king of spades.

If a cagey defender discards a spade, not a heart, baring his king, declarer must read the position. He will cash the ace-king of hearts, and when the queen does not drop, it is apparent the king of spades is now singleton.

Yes, I know *you* would discard a spade and then drop the queen of hearts on the second round to continue trying to give the impression of having started with 3-2-5-3 shape. But a West who is capable of those plays deserves to defeat the contract and win a *Bols* Brilliancy Prize.

My Tip for a Top

When playing in a notrump contract with the outstanding strength marked in one of the opponent's hands, reject the hold-up play in favor of the throw-in by retaining an exit card in the adversary's long suit.

Chapter 2

To Hold Up or Not To Hold Up, That is the Question

Questioning is not the mode of conversation among gentlemen.
Letter to James MacPherson, *Samuel Johnson*

In the last chapter, I described a situation where a hold-up play should be abandoned in favor of a throw-in because all the outstanding strength was known to be in the hand with the danger suit.

Here is another example of when the hold-up should be avoided. It is from a team game at our local club here in Mexico City.

Dlr: South
Vul: Both

♠ 8 7 2
♡ Q 9 5
◊ A K Q J 7
♣ A 10

♠ A J 5
♡ A J 10 8 3
◊ 6 4 2
♣ K J

West	North	East	South
			1 ♡
2 ♠ (a)	3 ◊ (b)	Pass	3NT (c)
Pass	6NT!	Pass	Pass
Pass			

(a) Weak   (b) Natural and forcing   (c) I can stop spades

The opening lead was the queen of spades, conventionally from a suit headed by the queen-jack or by the king-queen-ten and asking partner to jettison the jack or give count. How would you play the hand when East drops the three of spades at trick one?

My automatic reaction was to hold up, win the minor-suit shift and try the heart finesse sooner or later. If it was working, I would make my slam; if it lost, I was going down. But I paused to consider further. What about my opponent in the West seat? Did he favor making weak jump overcalls vulnerable with five-card suits, or only with six-carders; and would he consider king-queen-ten-sixth and out enough? Knowing this opponent well, I had some extra information. He was a solid character whose vulnerable two-spade bid was certain to be on a six-card suit (as emphasized by East's three). Therefore, I had an extra string to my bow. I won the first trick, crossed to dummy with a diamond and led the queen of hearts. When East played low, I rose with the ace, felling West's king and producing an overtrick. Obviously, if the finesse were working all along, I would have blown an overtrick, but the extra safety I gave myself was obviously worth it.

This was the full deal:

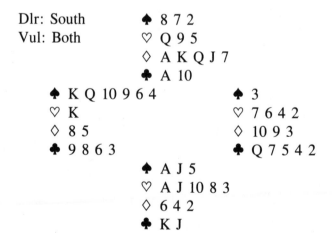

Dlr: South
Vul: Both

♠ 8 7 2
♡ Q 9 5
◇ A K Q J 7
♣ A 10

♠ K Q 10 9 6 4
♡ K
◇ 8 5
♣ 9 8 6 3

♠ 3
♡ 7 6 4 2
◇ 10 9 3
♣ Q 7 5 4 2

♠ A J 5
♡ A J 10 8 3
◇ 6 4 2
♣ K J

Interestingly, at one table the declarer went down in four hearts! He held up in spades at trick one, suffered a spade ruff at trick two, and finessed in hearts later, permitting a second spade ruff. He should have taken the safety-play in hearts too.

This hand is based on one given by the late Fred Karpin in *The Official Encyclopedia of Bridge*.

```
Dlr: South        ♠ K 8 6
Vul: Both         ♡ 6 3
                  ◊ A 10 8 7 6
                  ♣ K Q 4

                  ♠ A 7 5
                  ♡ A 7 5
                  ◊ Q J 9
                  ♣ A J 7 3
```

West	North	East	South
			1NT
Pass	3NT	Pass	Pass
Pass			

West leads the four of hearts; plan the play both at rubber bridge and matchpointed pairs.

At rubber bridge or IMPs it is clear that declarer should duck the ace of hearts for two rounds, and then take the diamond finesse. If it loses and East has another heart left, presumably the suit has broken 4-4 and the contract is safe. However, at matchpoints, if the diamond finesse is working, there are twelve tricks available, and it is possible other declarers will receive a different lead (West might be 4-4 in the majors, for example). In that case, they will make eleven or twelve tricks depending on the success of the finesse. Holding up the ace of hearts for two rounds leaves declarer unable to collect more than eleven tricks. Karpin suggests that the best play is to duck the first round and see what East returns. If he plays back the two, it is reasonable to assume that the hearts are 4-4, allowing declarer to win this trick with the king and take the diamond finesse. If, however, East returns, say, the ten of hearts, it is probably diplomatic to hold up the ace for one more round. With luck, this will be the full deal:

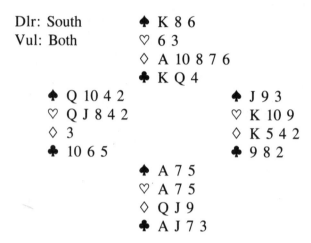

Dlr: South
Vul: Both

♠ K 8 6
♡ 6 3
♢ A 10 8 7 6
♣ K Q 4

♠ Q 10 4 2
♡ Q J 8 4 2
♢ 3
♣ 10 6 5

♠ J 9 3
♡ K 10 9
♢ K 5 4 2
♣ 9 8 2

♠ A 7 5
♡ A 7 5
♢ Q J 9
♣ A J 7 3

Those greedy declarers who win the second round of hearts will go down.

My Tip for a Top

Knowing the technique of the hold-up play is not enough; you must learn when to use it.

Chapter 3

Keeping Your Lines of Communication Open

Afoot and lighthearted I take to the open road,
Healthy, free, the world before me,
The long brown path before me leading wherever I choose.
                                  Song of the Open Road, *Walt Whitman*

My son Jerry is an electronics engineer and his speciality is telecommunications. We often share enthusiastic thoughts about the future: electronic mail, multi-way business conferences across continents, the office of tomorrow, and so on. However, at all times a poisonous cloud looms like a block to communications between people. Nations with opposing political ideologies are grimly facing each other; prejudiced minorities seek constant confrontations; the generation gap creates a schism within families. What is the solution to these serious and vexing problems? Even though there is not one panacea for all these ills, in my opinion a large step in the right direction is keeping the channels of communication open at any cost, so as to be able to disclose, discuss and discern the conflicting issues.

Problems of communication and blockage occur frequently in various disguises at the bridge table. Here is an example from a pair event:

```
Dlr: North        ♠ A K 7 6
Vul: Both         ♡ K J 5 2
                  ◇ K J
                  ♣ K Q J
    ♠ 5 3 2                      ♠ Q J 10 8
    ♡ Q 7                        ♡ A 8 4
    ◇ 10 9 6 4                   ◇ 8 7 2
    ♣ A 10 9 6                   ♣ 7 4 2
                  ♠ 9 4
                  ♡ 10 9 6 3
                  ◇ A Q 5 3
                  ♣ 8 5 3
```

After a conventional sequence, South had to play in four hearts, and West led the ten of diamonds.

The contract looks easy, and with the actual lie of the cards one would expect a competent declarer to bring home eleven tricks. However, watch how one player attacked the hand. He won the opening lead with dummy's jack, East giving the count. Wanting to draw trumps, declarer chose to cross to hand by cashing the ace-king of spades and ruffing the third round. However, when he ran the ten of hearts to East's ace, a fourth spade allowed West to overruff declarer with the queen of hearts and hold the contract to ten tricks: a below-average score for North-South.

Presumably you spotted the error in South's line. At trick one he should overtake the jack of diamonds with his queen, and then take the heart finesse. As the cards lie, the defense is helpless. If East ducks, another round of trumps brings down the queen, allowing declarer to win any return, draw the last trump and give up a club. If East wins the first round of hearts and returns a spade, declarer wins with dummy's king, cashes the king of diamonds and ace of spades, ruffs a spade in hand, plays off the ace of diamonds, discarding dummy's last spade, draws trumps and concedes a trick to the ace of clubs.

Curiously, even the inferior line taken by South could have

succeeded if he had cashed two rounds of diamonds and discarded dummy's last spade before running the ten of hearts. The best East can do after winning with the ace is to lead the ace and another club, locking declarer in the dummy, but the queen of hearts falls under the king and gives declarer eleven tricks.

As a final footnote: At teams you might consider winning the first trick in the dummy and leading a low heart!

This deal is an awkward bidding problem:

Dlr: North   ♠ A K 6 4
Vul: Both   ♡ A 5
                ◊ A J 9 5 4 2
                ♣ K

                ♠ 8 3 2
                ♡ 7 6
                ◊ Q 10 8
                ♣ A 8 7 4 2

West	North	East	South
	1 ◊	Pass	1NT
Pass	2 ♠	Pass	3 ◊
Pass	3 ♡	Pass	3NT
Pass	Pass	Pass	

West leads the queen of hearts; plan the play. Also, would you prefer to be in five diamonds?

In fact three notrump is the best game as it will make whenever the diamond finesse works. Five diamonds could still fail, losing a heart and two spade tricks or a spade overruff.

The chance of dropping a singleton king of diamonds in the East hand is only a little over six percent, so clearly the correct play is to win the first or second heart, overtake the king of clubs with the ace and run the ten or queen of diamonds, making the contract if the finesse works and going a lot down if it loses! (That is the plus of five diamonds: it is less expensive when East has the king of trumps.)

This was the full deal:

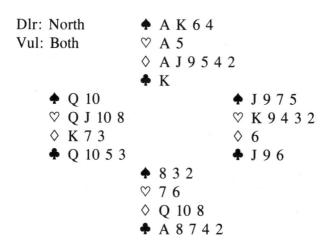

Dlr: North
Vul: Both

♠ A K 6 4
♡ A 5
◇ A J 9 5 4 2
♣ K

♠ Q 10
♡ Q J 10 8
◇ K 7 3
♣ Q 10 5 3

♠ J 9 7 5
♡ K 9 4 3 2
◇ 6
♣ J 9 6

♠ 8 3 2
♡ 7 6
◇ Q 10 8
♣ A 8 7 4 2

The best play is not difficult to recognize, but it does need some courage to be willing to risk a large penalty if a simple finesse is wrong.

My Tip for a Top

Watch your communications. Sometimes you may have to overtake a winner to keep your lines open.

164

Chapter 4

The Morton Fork

They sought it with thimbles, they sought with care;
   They pursued it with forks and hope;
They threatened its life with a railway-share;
   They charmed it with smiles and soap.

The Beaver's Lesson, Lewis Carroll

I often wonder why bridge writers invent fancy names for relatively simple plays, scaring the wits out of the uninitiated. The list of impressive-sounding coups is long and features names like the Scissors Coup, Devil's Coup, Vienna Coup, Deschapelles Coup and Grand Coup. One of these puzzling names in the Zoo of Bridge Plays is the *Morton's Fork Coup.* And just in case you are wondering who Mr. Morton is, was or will be, in fact he was Chancellor to Henry VII of England. He had a theory that nobles who had a high cost of living could obviously afford to pay taxes to the king, whereas those who lived frugally were clearly hoarding their money and so had a fair amount to spare for the king. A sort of "damned if I do and damned if I don't" situation. And yet behind this fantastic name hides a simple waiting play, postponing a discard on a winner until a defender has committed himself.

Here are two interesting example deals. The first cropped up during one of our weekly Wednesday games in Mexico City, in which I partnered my wife, Edith.

Dlr: East   ♠ K Q 6
Vul: Both   ♡ A 10 4
                ♦ A 8 5
                ♣ K Q 7 3

♠ 9 8 7 2   ♠ A J 10 4 3
♡ J 3   ♡ K 2
♦ 9 6 2   ♦ K J 10
♣ 8 6 5 4   ♣ A 10 9

                ♠ 5
                ♡ Q 9 8 7 6 5
                ♦ Q 7 4 3
                ♣ J 2

West	*North*	*East*	*South*
		1 ♠	Pass
Pass	Double	Redouble	3 ♡
Pass	4 ♡	Double	Pass
Pass	Pass		

I made a preemptive jump to three hearts, but Edith had a nice
hand and pushed me into game, hungrily doubled by East.

The opening lead was a spade, East winning dummy's king
with the ace. When East returned a spade I did not know what
to discard, so I ruffed the trick. I played a heart to the ace and
led a low club from the dummy. East was caught on the prongs
of Morton's Fork. If he rose with the ace, dummy would con-
tain three winners (the queen of spades and the top clubs) for
my diamond losers. And when instead he played low, I won
with the jack, crossed to the ace of diamonds, threw my club
loser on the queen of spades and led a trump. When East had
to win with the king, he was endplayed, and my third and last
loser was the king of diamonds.

I was given the second hand by Eddie Wold, who played it some
time ago in a Canadian Regional.

Dlr: West   ♠ A 5 2
Vul: E-W   ♡ A K 7
                 ◊ K 8 4
                 ♣ A 9 6 2

♠ J 9	♠ 7 6
♡ Q J 10 6 4 2	♡ 9 8 5 3
◊ A 9 2	◊ J 10 7 6
♣ 10 5	♣ Q J 8

                 ♠ K Q 10 8 4 3
                 ♡ —
                 ◊ Q 5 3
                 ♣ K 7 4 3

West	North	East	South
2♡	Double	Pass	3♡
Pass	3NT	Pass	4♠
Pass	6♠	Pass	Pass
Pass			

The opening lead was the queen of hearts, which declarer ruffed. Two rounds of trumps were drawn, and Wold judged that West was more likely to hold the ace of diamonds than East. So he led a diamond from hand toward the dummy. What could West do? If he rose with the ace, two club losers would go away on dummy's heart winners; and when he ducked, Wold won the trick with dummy's king, discarded his diamond losers on the hearts and played on clubs. When they broke 3-2 he was able to concede one trick and claim the slam.

My Tip for a Top

If you have available an early discard on a winner, consider postponing the decision. Try to visualize the layout of the opponents' hands, and consider if you may be able to impale one of them on Morton's Fork, the hypothetical trident of the Chancellor from the Middle Ages.

Chapter 5

Play for the Legitimate Chance, or Seek an Opponent's Error?

Es irrt der Mensch, so lang er strebt.

Man is in error throughout his life.
Faust, *Johann Wolfgang von Goethe*

You are moving into the expert category. You know, for example, the mathematical odds and have acquired the necessary tools for all the endplays. Coups, squeezes and dummy reversals are familiar territory to you. But how about your psychology? Do you play the same way against Bob Hamman or any other top expert as you do against lesser-known opponents? If you do, you are wrong!

A 'correct' technical play is sometimes better abandoned, especially if it offers little chance of success, in favor of creating an opportunity for the opponents to err.

In the following hand, my partner, Eddie Wold, was faced with a declarer-play problem against two experts. It occurred during the 1984 Blue Ribbon Pairs.

```
Dlr: South        ♠ 10 8 6
Vul: None         ♡ K J 5 2
                  ◇ K 8 7 2
                  ♣ K 6

                  ♠ J
                  ♡ A 8 4
                  ◇ Q J 10 9 5 3
                  ♣ A J 7
```

West	North	East	South
			1 ◇
1 ♠	Double (a)	2 ♠	3 ◇
Pass	5 ◇	Pass	Pass
Pass			

(a) Negative

The opening lead was the king of spades, on which East dropped a discouraging two. West switched to the six of hearts; how would you plan the play?

The obvious chance to avoid a heart loser was to propose to finesse the jack; normally a 50% chance. However, the defenders' plays made the odds favoring the finesse diminish considerably. East was known to have a high spade honor, yet he had discouraged; why? So Eddie decided to play for an error.

169

This was the full deal:

```
Dlr: South       ♠ 10 8 6
Vul: None        ♡ K J 5 2
                 ◊ K 8 7 2
                 ♣ K 6
  ♠ K Q 7 5 4 3           ♠ A 9 2
  ♡ 6 3                   ♡ Q 10 9 7
  ◊ 4                     ◊ A 6
  ♣ Q 9 8 2               ♣ 10 5 4 3
                 ♠ J
                 ♡ A 8 4
                 ◊ Q J 10 9 5 3
                 ♣ A J 7
```

Trick two was won with dummy's king of hearts and a low diamond led. East saw no danger in playing low, but it proved to be fatal. Eddie won with the queen, crossed to the king of clubs, ruffed a spade, cashed the ace of clubs, trumped a club in the dummy, ruffed dummy's last spade, and exited with a diamond to endplay East into leading away from his queen of hearts or conceding a ruff-and-discard.

A similar situation arose for me in an earlier event. This was the position that faced me:

Dlr: South   ♠ 10 8 6
Vul: Both   ♡ A K 10 8
                ◊ A 5
                ♣ 7 6 4 2

                ♠ A 3
                ♡ 7 6 2
                ◊ K 7
                ♣ A K Q J 10 8

I was in the ambitious contract of six notrump, against which West led the king of spades. How would you try to bring home twelve tricks?

The only legitimate chances appeared to be a double heart finesse, playing for West to hold both the queen and jack, or a major-suit squeeze against West, needing him to hold the three spade honors and any four hearts.

This was the actual full deal:

Dlr: South   ♠ 10 8 6
Vul: Both   ♡ A K 10 8
                ◊ A 5
                ♣ 7 6 4 2

♠ K Q J 9 2   ♠ 7 5 4
♡ Q 9 3   ♡ J 5 4
◊ 9 6 2   ◊ Q J 10 8 4 3
♣ 9 3   ♣ 5

                ♠ A 3
                ♡ 7 6 2
                ◊ K 7
                ♣ A K Q J 10 8

The squeeze seemed more likely, and so I ducked the first trick. West continued with the queen, I won with my ace and started to cash the clubs. On the first three rounds, West threw his two low spades and East discarded his three baby diamonds. But on the fourth round East began to feel the pinch. West parted with the two of diamonds, dummy shed the eight of hearts, but East did not want to release a diamond or a spade, so he jettisoned a seemingly useless heart.

That was all I needed. I cashed dummy's two red aces, returned to the king of diamonds and led my last club, squeezing West in the majors. Too late, East realized he should have thrown his third spade and held on to all his hearts.

Yes, I profited from a defensive error — perhaps one that *you* never would have made. But as the cards lay, that was the only way the slam could be brought home.

To end this chapter, a hand played in a major pair event by the Austrian, Peter Manhardt.

Dlr: North
Vul: E-W

♠ A 2
♥ A K Q 9 5
♦ 9 3
♣ K 10 8 7

♠ K 10 8 5
♥ J 10
♦ A Q 6 4 2
♣ J 6

West	North	East	South
	1 ♥	Pass	1 ♠
Pass	2 ♣	Pass	2NT
Pass	3NT	Pass	Pass
Pass			

West leads the queen of spades; what is your line of play?

After winning the first trick with dummy's ace, you probably decided to play on diamonds, finessing the queen at trick two. Even if it loses, West will be unable to play another spade. However, your hidden diamond suit might work to your advantage on an alternative approach. Manhardt led the seven of clubs from the dummy at trick two!

This was the full deal:

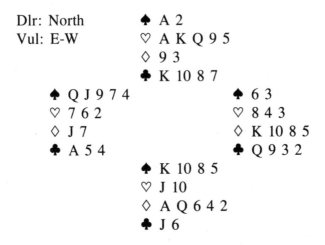

```
Dlr: North        ♠ A 2
Vul: E-W          ♡ A K Q 9 5
                  ◊ 9 3
                  ♣ K 10 8 7
    ♠ Q J 9 7 4              ♠ 6 3
    ♡ 7 6 2                  ♡ 8 4 3
    ◊ J 7                    ◊ K 10 8 5
    ♣ A 5 4                  ♣ Q 9 3 2
                  ♠ K 10 8 5
                  ♡ J 10
                  ◊ A Q 6 4 2
                  ♣ J 6
```

Not surprisingly, East did not go in with the queen of clubs, and so West had to win the trick with the ace. Now he erred by continuing with a low spade, declarer winning with the eight. A heart to the dummy, a successful diamond finesse, the king of spades and the rest of the hearts produced this position:

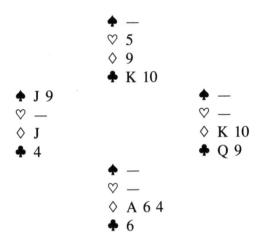

```
              ♠ —
              ♡ 5
              ◇ 9
              ♣ K 10
♠ J 9                        ♠ —
♡ —                         ♡ —
◇ J                         ◇ K 10
♣ 4                         ♣ Q 9
              ♠ —
              ♡ —
              ◇ A 6 4
              ♣ 6
```

The last heart squeezed East and declarer had brought home twelve tricks for a complete top.

In fact most declarers made only nine or ten tricks, playing three rounds of diamonds immediately, but Manhardt was likely to beat them once the club had got past East's queen. Suppose that West switches to the jack of diamonds at trick two. Declarer wins with the queen and starts to run the hearts, giving this end-position:

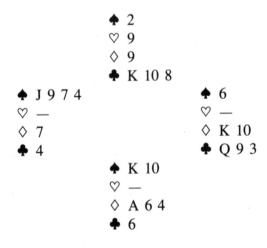

```
              ♠ 2
              ♡ 9
              ◇ 9
              ♣ K 10 8
♠ J 9 7 4                    ♠ 6
♡ —                         ♡ —
◇ 7                         ◇ K 10
♣ 4                         ♣ Q 9 3
              ♠ K 10
              ♡ —
              ◇ A 6 4
              ♣ 6
```

East is in an unenviable position when the last heart is led. He cannot avoid being endplayed in diamonds to lead away from the queen of clubs into dummy's tenace.

My Tip for a Top

When the legitimate chance for your contract is a low-percentage one, consider playing instead for a defensive error.

Chapter 6

Microscope or Telescope?
How Important is Knowing the Odds?

*The theory of probabilities is at the bottom nothing but
common sense reduced to Calculus.*
                                    Pierre Simon de Laplace

There are a few common misconceptions shared by a large part
of the bridge-playing population, particularly non-tournament
players. For example:

"To become an expert you have to be a good mathemati-
cian and know all about *exact* percentages."

"After a few tricks have been played, experts know how
all the cards are distributed."

The truth is quite different. Only a few experts have a pro-
found knowledge of mathematics. The late Ozzie Jacoby was
a wizard with numbers, and from the present generation in the
U.S. Dorothy Hayden and Alan Truscott and Jeff Rubens come
quickly to my mind. Most experts know the *approximate*
percentages but hardly anybody can tell the *exact* layout of the
cards after two or three tricks have been played.

The application of percentages can be particularly tricky. Not
only is there a difference between the a *priori* and the *a
posteriori* odds — that is, the expectations before the first card
is played and after the subsequent tricks — but also they apply
exactly only when *no inferences are available.* As Culbertson
reportedly said: "A gleam in an opponent's eye is worth more
than any percentage."

And the most important fact is often overlooked: *A percentage play which is correct for a suit taken in isolation may be
completely wrong in the context of the whole hand.*

Also, at the table there is generally not enough time available
to make exact calculations of the odds, so the Monday morn-

ing quarterback hindsight is reserved for the analysis of probabilities for different lines of play when you get home and can write down the actual figures.

Here is a hand that came up in our weekly matchpointed pair game.

Dlr: North
Vul: E-W

♠ K J 9 4
♡ A 7 3
♢ A 10 4
♣ J 8 5

♠ A 2
♡ Q J 8 6 4 2
♢ K 9
♣ Q 10 3

West	North	East	South
	1 ♣	Pass	1 ♡
Pass	1 ♠	Pass	2 ♢
Pass	2 ♡	Pass	4 ♡
Pass	Pass	Pass	

The opening lead is the jack of diamonds; what is your line of play after winning the first trick in hand with the king?

It looks like a simple hand hinging around the play of the trump suit. Finding the king of hearts doubleton onside is a 20% chance according to the tables. Leading low to the ace wins whenever the king is singleton (12.5%) or when East has all four trumps (5%).

An advantage of 2.5% is nothing to be sneezed out, but look before you leap: *consider the whole hand.* What about the opening lead of the jack of diamonds? As the ten is in the dummy, it must be from shortness. True, a 7-1 distribution of the diamonds is unlikely (1.5%), but if the lead is honest, the percentages have changed dramatically as the diamonds must be breaking either 1-7 or 2-6. And this alters the odds in the heart suit. The probability of East's holding a singleton king has increased; though, on the down side, the chances of his holding all four hearts have dropped considerably. Furthermore, what about the club suit? If they do not break 4-3 (*a priori* 37.8%), the opponents may discover their club ruff if the heart finesse fails. Of course they might have found the ruff immediately, but that was very unlikely in view of the one-club opening bid.

Looking at the whole hand with a telescope instead of a microscope, the odds have shifted in favor of playing a heart to the ace and one back. And this was what one declarer did; though I expect he was momentarily apprehensive, worried that West would have king-doubleton all along. However, East did win the second round with the king and everyone followed.

That seemed to be that, but suddenly there was a surprise for South. East started thinking, and after a long pause, even though his partner had not echoed to show three trumps, he returned the two of diamonds! West discarded the nine of clubs, and dummy won with the ten. Suddenly declarer, after worrying about defeat, was able to consider making an overtrick.

West was known to have started with three red cards and ten black, whereas East had nine red and four black. So the possibility of a black-suit squeeze on West was obvious. Declarer cashed dummy's other diamond winner and then ran his trumps.

With one round to go, this was the position:

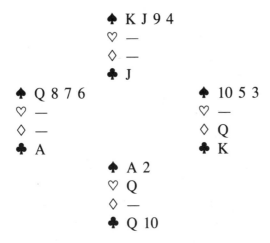

♠ K J 9 4
♥ —
♦ —
♣ J

♠ Q 8 7 6   ♠ 10 5 3
♥ —   ♥ —
♦ —   ♦ Q
♣ A   ♣ K

♠ A 2
♥ Q
♦ —
♣ Q 10

West did well to discard the ace of clubs on the last heart, but declarer still finessed the jack of spades and made an overtrick for a shared top. Many players went one down, and some even finished two down after taking a trump finesse and walking into a crossruff.

This was the full deal:

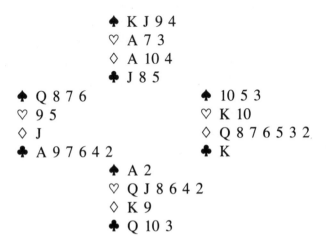

```
              ♠ K J 9 4
              ♡ A 7 3
              ◇ A 10 4
              ♣ J 8 5
♠ Q 8 7 6                    ♠ 10 5 3
♡ 9 5                        ♡ K 10
◇ J                          ◇ Q 8 7 6 5 3 2
♣ A 9 7 6 4 2                ♣ K
              ♠ A 2
              ♡ Q J 8 6 4 2
              ◇ K 9
              ♣ Q 10 3
```

Clearly, if East cashes the king of clubs at trick four, declarer can organize a black-suit squeeze against West. And it is interesting to consider what would have happened if at trick four East had returned a low spade. Declarer runs it to dummy's nine (West had better not put up the queen!), cashes the ace of diamonds, ruffs a diamond, plays off the ace of spades and leads a low club in this position:

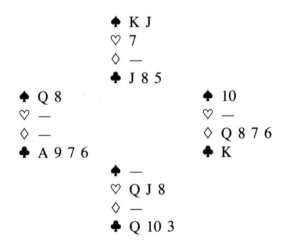

```
              ♠ K J
              ♡ 7
              ◇ —
              ♣ J 8 5
♠ Q 8                        ♠ 10
♡ —                          ♡ —
◇ —                          ◇ Q 8 7 6
♣ A 9 7 6                    ♣ K
              ♠ —
              ♡ Q J 8
              ◇ —
              ♣ Q 10 3
```

West cannot rise with the ace without conceding an overtrick, but when East wins with the king he is endplayed. A diamond return is ruffed in the dummy while declarer discards a club, and the last club disappears on the king of spades. Whereas a spade is into dummy's tenace and again allows declarer to divest himself of his club losers.

Here is another hand with several possible lines of play. It was board three of round three in the 1985 Bermuda Bowl and Venice Cup in São Paulo, Brazil.

```
Dlr: East          ♠ 10 9 7 5 2
Vul: N-S           ♡ 5
                   ◇ 7 4 3
                   ♣ A K 9 3

                   ♠ A Q J 6 4 3
                   ♡ A K 6
                   ◇ K 6 2
                   ♣ 5
```

West	North	East	South
			1 ♠
Pass	4 ♠	Pass	4NT (a)
Pass	5 ◇ (b)	Pass	5 ♠
Pass	Pass	Pass	

(a) Roman Key Card Blackwood   (b) One of the five 'aces'

West leads the jack of hearts; what is your line?

At the time, two players cashed the ace of spades at trick two. By my calculations, that line succeeds some 86% of the time. One South crossed to the dummy and led a spade, finessing the queen when East contributed the eight. That line is around 83%. And one declarer went for a partial elimination, playing off three rounds of clubs and hearts, discarding *diamonds* from both hands, before taking the spade finesse. This will make the contract about 82% of the time.

This was the actual full deal:

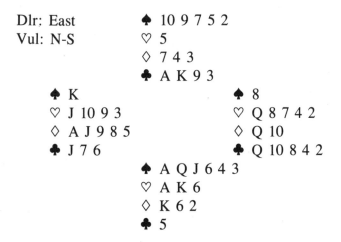

Dlr: East
Vul: N-S

```
                ♠ 10 9 7 5 2
                ♡ 5
                ◊ 7 4 3
                ♣ A K 9 3
   ♠ K                         ♠ 8
   ♡ J 10 9 3                  ♡ Q 8 7 4 2
   ◊ A J 9 8 5                 ◊ Q 10
   ♣ J 7 6                     ♣ Q 10 8 4 2
                ♠ A Q J 6 4 3
                ♡ A K 6
                ◊ K 6 2
                ♣ 5
```

As you can see, only the line of taking an immediate finesse fails as the cards lie. But the best line proved elusive to the players. You should try for a total elimination: win with the ace of hearts, cash the king, discarding a *club* from dummy, play three rounds of clubs, ruffing the last in hand, trump the six of hearts in the dummy and finesse the queen of spades. This line has some 90% chance of success.

Not that this proves a lot, except how difficult it can be to decide between four lines of play that are all reasonable. Which did you choose?

My next hand, from the 1987 Spring Nationals in St. Louis, also revolves around the trump suit:

Dlr: South   ♠ K 8 7 4
Vul: E-W   ♡ J 6 2
              ◊ A Q J 3
              ♣ 10 5

              ♠ A 3
              ♡ A 10 7 5 4 3
              ◊ K 5 2
              ♣ Q 2

West	North	East	South
			1 ♡
Pass	1 ♠	Pass	2 ♡
Pass	3 ♡	Pass	4 ♡
Pass	Pass	Pass	

West leads the two of spades. You win with dummy's king and lead a low trump, East contributing the eight. What do you do now?

There are three possibilities this time:

a. Finesse the ten.

b. Rise with the ace and, if West plays low, continue with a second round of hearts.

c. Rise with the ace and, if West plays low, switch to diamonds in the hope of being able to discard a club loser.

Which is your choice?

The actual odds of the two plays in the trump suit are equal, but the advantage of putting in the ten is that you stand some chance of survival if East has all four hearts. Also, though this probability is minuscule, as West did not lead a club at trick one, he *might* not switch to the suit if he wins trick two.

This was the actual full deal:

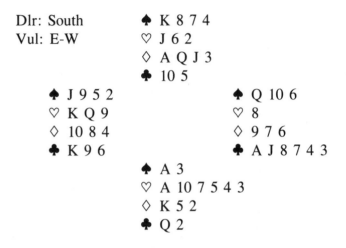

```
Dlr: South        ♠ K 8 7 4
Vul: E-W          ♡ J 6 2
                  ◇ A Q J 3
                  ♣ 10 5
     ♠ J 9 5 2                    ♠ Q 10 6
     ♡ K Q 9                      ♡ 8
     ◇ 10 8 4                     ◇ 9 7 6
     ♣ K 9 6                      ♣ A J 8 7 4 3
                  ♠ A 3
                  ♡ A 10 7 5 4 3
                  ◇ K 5 2
                  ♣ Q 2
```

The fact that line *b* works is besides the point. Actually it is mathematically worse than *c* because if we assume the spades to be 3-4 or 4-3 and the hearts to be 3-1, the person short in hearts is more likely to be long in diamonds. He has eight or nine 'holes' in which to put those diamonds, whereas his partner has only six or seven 'holes' available.

My Tip for a Top

Acquire a general knowledge of percentages, but look at the hand as a whole, not just at one suit; and be ready to abandon percentage plays if inferences so dictate. Also, remember that shortness can alter the *a priori* odds significantly.

Chapter 7

Finding the Lady

Knowledge is of two kinds. We know the subject ourselves,
or we know where to find information upon it.

Samuel Johnson

"If there is anything mysterious in a man's behavior, *cherchons la femme.*" Alexandre Dumas, in *The Mohicans of Paris*, cited this morsel of wisdom of Joseph Fouché, Chief of Paris Police during the Directorate. He did not say how, but bridge experts enjoy the reputation of having an uncanny ability to locate Her Royal Highness when faced with a two-way finesse.

Playing as Oswald Jacoby's partner for the first time, Barry Crane discussed this problem.

"I've been playing that mathematically there is a slight advantage to the theory that the queen lies over the jack."

"Not so," pronounced the wizard of odds. "It doesn't make any difference, as long as you always play it the same way."

"All right," conceded Crane, though not entirely convinced. "Then I'll play 'over the jack' in minor suits and 'under the jack' in the majors."

On one occasion, no less a personage than auction great Wilbur C. Whitehead devised a surer method. Suspecting that the queen was held by the l.o.l. on his left, he patted her hand and said, "You look like a lady with the queen of trumps."

"Oh, Mr. Whitehead," she gushed. "Aren't you wonderful!"

Hal Sims, giant of the early '30s, claimed that he could "always" find a missing queen by observing carefully the behavior of his opponents. His friends decided to deflate this boast by stacking a deck to put the queen of trumps in the hand of each defender. After long study, Sims seemed to be foiled. "Dammit," he declared, "there must be *two* trump queens in this deck!"

Few players are born with this rare gift, and table presence cannot be taught. But there is plenty of advice in the vast literature on play, commencing with Watson, Culbertson, Brown and Goren, and progressing to more recent authorities, including Kaplan, Kelsey, Mollo, Reese and, lately, Lawrence and Stewart. You will soon learn that the most important element of card-reading is counting. I do not propose to cover this primary tool, other than to remind you that counting must include both high-card points and distribution.

Here are three examples of apparent guesses that will show you what is possible after some practice and application at the table.

1.

Dlr: North
Vul: None

       ♠ 9 4 3
       ♡ K 6 5 3 2
       ◇ 10 7 3
       ♣ 10 9

       ♠ 10
       ♡ A J 10 9 4
       ◇ K 8 2
       ♣ A K 7 5

West	North	East	South
	Pass	Pass	1 ♡
Pass	Pass	1 ♠	2 ♣
2 ♠	3 ♡	3 ♠	Double (a)
Pass	4 ♡	Pass	Pass
Pass			

(a) It is matchpoints!

West leads the king of spades and East (incorrectly and discourteously) tosses the queen onto the table before you have called for a card from the dummy. What is your line of play after West continues with another spade?

2.

Dlr: South
Vul: N-S

♠ J 10 9 4
♡ 10 6
◊ K Q 3 2
♣ Q J 7

♠ A K 8 3
♡ 8 7 4
◊ A J 5
♣ K 6 4

West	North	East	South
			1NT
2♡	3♡ (a)	Pass	3♠
Pass	4♠	Pass	Pass
Pass			

(a) Stayman

West starts with the king and queen of hearts, East echoing with the nine and two. However, West ignores his partner's signal and switches to the nine of clubs at trick three, won with East's ace. When the two of clubs comes back and West follows, how do you continue?

3.

Dlr: North
Vul: N-S

♠ A 8 6 4
♡ K 10 8 4
◇ A 8 6
♣ K 2

♠ Q J
♡ A J 5 2
◇ Q 4 3
♣ Q 5 4 3

West	North	East	South
Meckstroth	*Sekhar*	*Johnson*	*Cannell*
	1NT (a)	Pass	2♣
2 ◇	3 ◇ (b)	Pass	4 ♡
Pass	Pass	Pass	

(a) 13-15 points   (b) Maximum with two four-card majors

West leads the three of spades, third best, you play low from the dummy and East wins with the king. Back comes the two of diamonds, and you take West's ten with dummy's ace. You cross to the queen of spades, play a heart to the king, discard a diamond on the ace of spades, ruff dummy's last spade, East throwing a diamond, lead a club to the king and duck a club, taken with West's jack. West continues with the ace of clubs, which you ruff in the dummy. What now?

4.

Dlr: North
Vul: None

♠ A J 9 3
♡ A Q
◊ K 7 2
♣ 8 6 5 4

♠ K 10 7 4
♡ K J 4
◊ A 5 4
♣ K Q J

West	North	East	South
	1 ♣	Pass	1 ♠
Pass	2 ♠	Pass	4NT
Pass	5 ♡	Pass	6 ♠
Pass	Pass	Pass	

West leads the three of diamonds; which opponent has the queen of spades?

This is what happened at the table, supplemented with the full deals. In the first I was South, and mentally congratulated my partner for removing my double of three spades.

Dlr: North
Vul: None

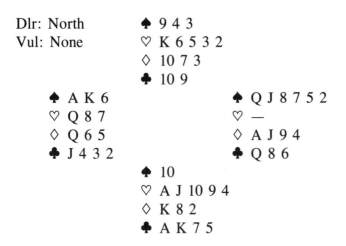

```
                    ♠ 9 4 3
                    ♡ K 6 5 3 2
                    ◊ 10 7 3
                    ♣ 10 9
    ♠ A K 6                         ♠ Q J 8 7 5 2
    ♡ Q 8 7                         ♡ —
    ◊ Q 6 5                         ◊ A J 9 4
    ♣ J 4 3 2                       ♣ Q 8 6
                    ♠ 10
                    ♡ A J 10 9 4
                    ◊ K 8 2
                    ♣ A K 7 5
```

In four hearts, I had to assume that East had the ace of diamonds; and it appeared that West had the ace and king of spades. My only problem was a 3-0 trump break, and because of his original pass and later aggressive bidding, it seemed likely that if anyone were void in hearts, it would be East. So I ruffed the spade continuation and laid down the ace of trumps. When East showed out, making ten tricks proved easy.

The key to the second deal is asking oneself why West ignored his partner's signal in hearts and shifted to a club. Eddie Wold correctly deduced that West knew his partner could not overruff the dummy on the third round of hearts.

190

This was the full deal:

```
Dlr: South          ♠ J 10 9 4
Vul: N-S            ♡ 10 6
                    ◇ K Q 3 2
                    ♣ Q J 7
    ♠ Q 2                        ♠ 7 6 5
    ♡ A K Q J 5 3                ♡ 9 2
    ◇ 9 6                        ◇ 10 8 7 4
    ♣ 9 8 5                      ♣ A 10 3 2
                    ♠ A K 8 3
                    ♡ 8 7 4
                    ◇ A J 5
                    ♣ K 6 4
```

Backing his judgment, Wold played off the ace and king of spades, dropping West's queen.

The third deal helped North-South, G. Sekhar (he never uses his first name!) and Drew Cannell, to win the 1986 Grand National Pairs.

This was the full distribution:

```
Dlr: North          ♠ A 8 6 4
Vul: N-S            ♡ K 10 8 4
                    ◇ A 8 6
                    ♣ K 2
    ♠ 10 7 3 2                   ♠ K 9 5
    ♡ Q 6                        ♡ 9 7 3
    ◇ K J 10 7                   ◇ 9 5 2
    ♣ A J 8                      ♣ 10 9 7 6
                    ♠ Q J
                    ♡ A J 5 2
                    ◇ Q 4 3
                    ♣ Q 5 4 3
```

After the first eight tricks, Meckstroth could have exited with the king and another diamond, putting declarer in his hand. Cannell could then get into the dummy by ruffing a club, but that would appear risky and probably tempt him to lay down the ace of hearts, with gratifying results. So Meckstroth led the ace of clubs, forcing declarer into the dummy. But Cannell worked out why Meckstroth was being so 'sporting' — he played a heart to the ace, dropping the queen, and claimed his contract.

The fourth hand is nearly 25 years old. I was playing with Jim Jacoby against Alan Truscott, who had only just arrived from England to take the job of Executive Editor for the first edition of *The Official Encyclopedia of Bridge*.

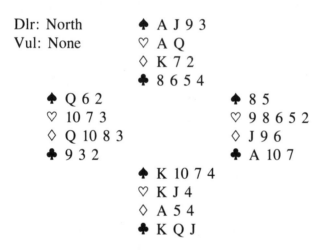

Dlr: North
Vul: None

```
                    ♠ A J 9 3
                    ♡ A Q
                    ◇ K 7 2
                    ♣ 8 6 5 4
    ♠ Q 6 2                        ♠ 8 5
    ♡ 10 7 3                       ♡ 9 8 6 5 2
    ◇ Q 10 8 3                     ◇ J 9 6
    ♣ 9 3 2                        ♣ A 10 7
                    ♠ K 10 7 4
                    ♡ K J 4
                    ◇ A 5 4
                    ♣ K Q J
```

I won the opening diamond lead in hand, crossed to the ace of spades and finessed through East for the queen of spades, thus losing my slam and the Life Masters Pairs title at the same time.

"Obviously you haven't heard of Truscott's rule," remarked Alan.

"What's that?" I asked, somewhat miffed.

"When you have nothing else to go by, the queen of trumps is always on declarer's left."

My shocked expression brought this explanation: "This isn't like the superstition that the queen always lies over the jack. It's based on the fact that, with a blind opening lead, left-hand opponent might well have chosen a trump from an unimportant holding. His failure to do so slightly increases the chances that he holds the queen."

Having followed this principle through all the intervening years, I can confirm its soundness. And, more important than bringing me this wise rule, it started a rewarding friendship.

My Tip for a Top

To locate a crucial queen, count, use psychology and whatever inferences you can from the bidding and play. If still uncertain, apply 'Truscott's Rule'.

Chapter 8

Establish a Long Suit or Play for Ruffs?

La justice est la sanction des injustices établies

Justice is the means by which established injustices
are sanctioned.

Crainquebille, *Anatole France*

Even accomplished players are sometimes vexed by the problem of whether to establish dummy's suit or to take ruffs in the dummy. In my experience, the large majority of declarers automatically go for the ruffs, especially if dummy is the short trump hand. But bridge teachers often warn their students that, in most cases, it is better to try to establish the long suit. Who is right?

Before I give an answer, consider this example from *Goren on Play and Defense*:

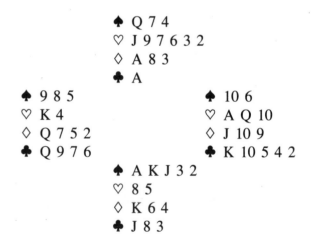

```
                  ♠ Q 7 4
                  ♡ J 9 7 6 3 2
                  ◇ A 8 3
                  ♣ A
    ♠ 9 8 5                      ♠ 10 6
    ♡ K 4                        ♡ A Q 10
    ◇ Q 7 5 2                    ◇ J 10 9
    ♣ Q 9 7 6                    ♣ K 10 5 4 2
                  ♠ A K J 3 2
                  ♡ 8 5
                  ◇ K 6 4
                  ♣ J 8 3
```

The contract is four spades and a diamond is led. There are eight likely winners: five trumps, the ace and king of diamonds and the ace of clubs. To bring himself up to ten tricks, South may try either to ruff two clubs in the dummy or to establish the heart suit.

Suppose South goes for the club ruffs. In that case, he will need entries to his hand, and so must win the opening lead with dummy's ace. He cashes the ace of clubs, crosses to the king of diamonds, ruffs a club, plays a spade to the ace and trumps his last club, this time with the queen of spades.

So far everything has gone well, but there are storm signals in the air, declarer having no way back to hand to draw the remaining trumps. No matter what he leads next, the defenders will be able to cash two hearts and a diamond. If West has the lead, he can play his last diamond, which East will ruff with the ten of spades to promote a trump trick for his partner. If East is on lead, his third heart will again produce a spade trick for his partner.

What South learns from the experience is that the ruffing play does not work for lack of entries to his own hand. So he should now consider whether dummy has enough entries to allow the hearts to be established. This time South wins the diamond lead in hand, plays a heart, wins the diamond return and concedes another heart. Suppose that the opponents now cash a diamond trick and shift to a club. A heart is ruffed high in hand (as East produces the last heart) and three rounds of trumps are drawn ending in the dummy. With the majors both breaking 3-2, the contract is made. Clearly, the suit-establishment play is superior. (Against a club lead, declarer should also play to establish the hearts. Though, if the defenders keep plugging away with clubs, he may change horses and ruff the two losers in the dummy.)

Now let us change the hand slightly, switching the ace and jack of clubs.

```
              ♠ Q 7 4
              ♡ J 9 7 6 3 2
              ◊ A 8 3
              ♣ J
♠ 9 8 5                        ♠ 10 6
♡ K 4                          ♡ A Q 10
◊ Q 7 5 2                      ◊ J 10 9
♣ Q 9 7 6                      ♣ K 10 5 4 2
              ♠ A K J 3 2
              ♡ 8 5
              ◊ K 6 4
              ♣ A 8 3
```

If declarer tries to establish the heart suit, he wins the diamond lead in hand, plays a heart, wins the diamond return, plays another heart, loses a diamond trick and wins the club exit in hand. He cannot get to dummy, establish the hearts, draw trumps and get back to the dummy to run the winners. Too bad.

But with this swap of the club honors, the ruffing line works. Declarer wins the diamond lead in the dummy, plays a club to the ace, ruffs a club, crosses to the king of diamonds, ruffs his last club and cashes the queen of spades. Now he can cast adrift and at worst be forced to ruff something high and play for the spades to be 3-2. (Declarer might ruff the last club high and try to draw trumps immediately, but it is unnecessary; he might still be able to make the contract with the trumps breaking 4-1.)

Is someone suggesting that a trump lead is fatal? Not so, because now declarer has two alternatives. The more complicated is to revert to the suit-establishment line! Win the trump lead in hand and concede a heart. Take the expected trump return (or diamond switch) in hand and give up a second heart. No matter what the defenders do, there are three entries left in the dummy — just enough to draw the remaining trump, establish the hearts and get back to the dummy to cash them. This line even produces an overtrick!

The simpler approach is to win the trump lead with dummy's queen, play a club to the ace, ruff a club, return to the king of diamonds, ruff the last club and exit with two rounds of diamonds. Declarer will be able to ruff the third round of hearts high and draw trumps, making ten tricks in all.

Now we can answer the question posed at the beginning:

My Tip for a Top

When there is a choice between playing to establish dummy's suit and ruffing losers in the dummy, declarer should follow this principle: With excellent entries to the closed hand, go for ruffs in the dummy; with sufficient entries in the opposite hand, plan to establish dummy's suit.

Chapter 9

Can You Afford a Safety Play?

Out of this nettle, danger, we pluck this flower, safety.
Henry IV, Part 1, *William Shakespeare*

Duplicate players are generally not too concerned with safety plays when they are competing for matchpoints rather than money. Yet even in a pairs game safety plays can be important: usually when you are in a good contract that other pairs are unlikely to reach. The problem is that often you cannot know how to tackle a particular holding which lends itself to a safety play because it depends upon the number of losers in a side suit.

In spite of the fact that this theme has been presented repeatedly by different authors, somehow occasionally even experienced players tend to ignore it. Here are two examples from the weekly duplicate game at our club.

Dlr: South   ♠ A Q 5 4
Vul: Both   ♡ A Q 3
              ◊ K 5 4
              ♣ Q 3 2

              ♠ 9 8 7 6 3
              ♡ 10 4
              ◊ A Q J
              ♣ A K 4

South opened one spade, and later found himself in six spades. West led the jack of clubs; how would you play the hand?

At the table the declarer immediately finessed the queen of spades. Unfortunately, this lost to the singleton king and, although West had the king of hearts, he had to go one down.

This was the full deal:

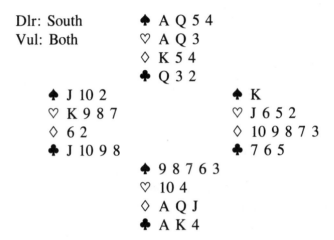

Dlr: South
Vul: Both

♠ A Q 5 4
♡ A Q 3
◇ K 5 4
♣ Q 3 2

♠ J 10 2
♡ K 9 8 7
◇ 6 2
♣ J 10 9 8

♠ K
♡ J 6 5 2
◇ 10 9 8 7 3
♣ 7 6 5

♠ 9 8 7 6 3
♡ 10 4
◇ A Q J
♣ A K 4

Where did declarer go wrong? At trick two, before tackling the trumps, he should have taken the heart finesse to clarify the position in that suit. If it loses, he has to play West for the king-doubleton in spades. However, when it wins, declarer should safety play the trumps by cashing the ace first to protect against the actual situation of a singleton king *chez* East.

What about the possible overtrick? That is only a 20% shot, and should be rejected in favor of the 78% chance of making the contract by playing the spades in the suggested way.

Here is the second problem:

Dlr: South
Vul: E-W

♠ J 7 4
♡ A 4 2
◊ A K J 2
♣ K J 3

♠ A K 6 5 3
♡ K 5
◊ 8 7 4
♣ A 10 6

Once more the contract was six spades, and West led the jack of hearts. What is your plan of campaign?

This time the actual declarer, apparently not benefiting from the previous hand, won with the ace in the dummy and cashed his two top spades. He was elated to see the queen drop doubleton from East, so he drew the last trump, cashed the ace of diamonds, crossed back to hand with a heart to the king and took the diamond finesse. East won with the queen and forced declarer with a heart. Next came a diamond, but West had both of the last two, and so South was forced into guessing the location of the queen of clubs. Even though West was known to have seven cards in spades and diamonds to East's four, declarer decided East would not have begun with all four queens, so he played West for that card and went one down.

This was the full deal:

Dlr: South
Vul: E-W

```
                    ♠ J 7 4
                    ♡ A 4 2
                    ◇ A K J 2
                    ♣ K J 3
   ♠ 10 8 2                        ♠ Q 9
   ♡ J 10 8                        ♡ Q 9 7 6 3
   ◇ 10 9 6 5                      ◇ Q 3
   ♣ 9 8 4                         ♣ Q 7 5 2
                    ♠ A K 6 5 3
                    ♡ K 5
                    ◇ 8 7 4
                    ♣ A 10 6
```

One might disagree with South's view in the club suit, but his earlier play is more open to criticism. After the luck in the spade suit, he should have taken the safety play in diamonds of cashing the ace *and* king. If the queen does not drop, he crosses to the king of hearts and leads a diamond toward the dummy. Only if East started with queen-fourth of diamonds will declarer be reduced to finding the queen of clubs; and then no play in diamonds would help.

My Tip for a Top

In order to decide whether or not you can afford a safety play in a suit, first find out how many losers you have in the critical side suit.

Chapter 10

The Cutting Edge or Cutting the Edge

Progress has its drawbacks and they are great and serious.
Liberty, Equality and Fraternity, *Sir James Fitzjames Stephen*

I find the most recent trend in bidding disconcerting. First there were the 'fertilizer' bids from New Zealand, used in conjunction with a strong pass system. As a pass in the first or second position shows positive values, these players have to open when holding few points; and these weak openings came to be called fertilizer bids, or ferts for short. These systems are not permitted in North America, but always looking for an edge, 'garbage' preempts are now in fashion. The Multicolored two-diamond opening, showing a weak two-bid in either major or some variety of stronger hand, has been popular in Britain for many years, but has only just reared its head on this side of the Atlantic. And as it releases two-heart and two-spade openings for alternative interpretations, a Pandora's box of preempts has been perforated. Two hearts is often used to show four cards in that suit with a longer minor; two spades may be a weak preempt in an unspecified suit; or it may be a weak two-suiter including spades; two notrump could be any weak one-suiter with three-level openings being transfer preempts promising respectable suits; and so on.

I predict this fashion will last only until players have learned how to defend effectively against these methods; and then they will rapidly vanish into oblivion.

Fortunately the *nouvelle vogue* has not hit Mexico yet, but undisciplined weak twos are taking their toll amongst the inexperienced players in our club. Miguel Reygadas and I were practicing for the forthcoming Grand Nationals when this hand arose. My left-hand opponent was one of my talented pupils, extremely aggressive in her exuberant youth, and my RHO was her mother, a seasoned Mexican international.

Sitting South as dealer with neither side vulnerable, I picked up

♠ A 5 2   ♡ Q J 10 9 8 7 5   ♢ 4   ♣ J 3

In contrast to the modern trend, I do not like to preempt first-in-hand; and I am even less fond of the idea when holding an outside ace. My first- and second-seat weak twos and threes are very disciplined. I prefer to bid my cards accurately and not make my prime aim to try to steal the opponents blind. Call me old-fashioned if you wish, but I passed.

A cheerful, ''Skip bid; two spades,'' on my left. Miguel passed after the mandatory ten-second pause. And my RHO bid a forcing three diamonds. It was now time to introduce my seven-card heart suit. Two passes were followed by a resolute double (obviously for penalties) on my right. My young pupil seemed happy with the state of affairs, but Miguel was clearly not so pleased.

The opening lead was the ten of diamonds, and this was what I could see:

```
Dlr: South        ♠ Q 10 3
Vul: None         ♡ 6
                  ◇ Q J 5 3
                  ♣ A 10 8 5 2


                  ♠ A 5 2
                  ♡ Q J 10 9 8 7 5
                  ◇ 4
                  ♣ J 3
```

West	North	East	South
			Pass
2♠	Pass	3◇	3♡
Pass	Pass	Double	Pass
Pass	Pass		

Not too bad, I thought; with luck I will get out with eight tricks. I covered the ten of diamonds with the jack and East won with the king. The next card to hit the table was an unbelievable king of spades! So my pupil had opened two spades in the second seat with jack-nine-sixth, or maybe even only -fifth!

I won with my ace and led the jack of hearts, everyone following and East winning with the king. After some thought, she switched to the six of clubs, obviously hoping she could get her daughter on lead in clubs and obtain a spade ruff. But I had a countermeasure available. I won with dummy's ace and led the queen of diamonds, discarding my jack of clubs when East produced the ace. Like Little Tommy Tucker in the old nursery rhyme, I had cut their communications without a knife. The Scissors Coup, a relatively rare play, had rendered the opposition helpless. After ruffing the club return, I knocked out the ace of hearts, regained the lead, drew trumps and finessed the ten of spades to land my contract.

This was the complete deal:

```
Dlr: South        ♠ Q 10 3
Vul: None         ♡ 6
                  ◊ Q J 5 3
                  ♣ A 10 8 5 2
    ♠ J 9 8 7 6 4         ♠ K
    ♡ 2                   ♡ A K 4 3
    ◊ 10 6                ◊ A K 9 8 7 2
    ♣ K Q 9 7             ♣ 6 4
                  ♠ A 5 2
                  ♡ Q J 10 9 8 7 5
                  ◊ 4
                  ♣ J 3
```

How would you play this hand?

```
Dlr: North        ♠ 5
Vul: E-W          ♡ 8 7 6
                  ◊ J 9 8 7 6 5 3
                  ♣ J 6

                  ♠ Q J 8 4 3 2
                  ♡ 4
                  ◊ —
                  ♣ A K Q 8 3 2
```

West	North	East	South
	Pass	1 ♡	2 ♡ (a)
3 ♡	Pass	4 ♡	4 ♠
Double	Pass	Pass	Pass

(a) Michaels Cue-Bid

West leads the king of diamonds; what is your line of play?

This board cropped up during the semifinals of the 1987 Grand National Teams, won for the fourth time in six years by Chip Martel-Lew Stansby and Peter Pender-Hugh Ross, and assisted by Mike Lawrence.

This was the full deal:

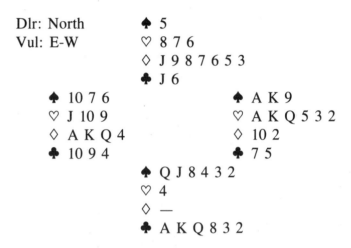

Dlr: North
Vul: E-W

```
                    ♠ 5
                    ♡ 8 7 6
                    ◊ J 9 8 7 6 5 3
                    ♣ J 6
   ♠ 10 7 6                        ♠ A K 9
   ♡ J 10 9                        ♡ A K Q 5 3 2
   ◊ A K Q 4                       ◊ 10 2
   ♣ 10 9 4                        ♣ 7 5
                    ♠ Q J 8 4 3 2
                    ♡ 4
                    ◊ —
                    ♣ A K Q 8 3 2
```

In the other room, the auction went as follows:

West	North	East	South
Rodwell	Martel	Meckstroth	Stansby
	3 ◊ !	Double	4 ♠
Double	Pass	Pass	5 ♣
Double	Pass	Pass	Pass

That preemptive opening bid is not characteristic of Martel (or any of his team-mates). And then Stansby chose to run from four spades doubled to the hoped-for safety of his stronger suit.

Rodwell led the king of diamonds, declarer ruffed, drew two rounds of trumps ending in the dummy and played a spade. Meckstroth went up with the king, cashed the king of hearts and forced declarer with a second round of the suit. Stansby drew the last trump, knocked out the ace of spades, took another force with his final trump and led the jack of spades. Luckily the suit was 3-3 and so he finished one, not four, down.

The declarer in four spades doubled was David Caslan, playing for Indiana. He ruffed the diamond lead, crossed to the dummy's jack of clubs and led a spade. However, East, Hugh Ross, went in with the king and returned his second club. When Ross got in with the ace of spades he underled his heart honors to partner's nine and received a club ruff to defeat the contract and achieve a flat board. If only declarer has discarded his heart at trick one, he would have made four spades doubled.

What a rarity, making a Scissors Coup at trick one when holding a 6-6-1-0 shape!

This time two of my tips really fit in the bidding section; but it does not hurt to show that the three parts of bridge are inextricably entwined.

My Tip for a Top

1. Do not open a weak two-bid unless you can stand partner to lead the suit from king singleton or doubleton.
2. Do not preempt in the first or second seat at the three-level or higher with an outside ace.
3. If the opponents seem to be going after ruffs, think about cutting their communications with a loser-on-loser play: the Scissors Coup. This maneuver with the fancy name is not only the expert's privilege.

Chapter 11

Know Your Weaknesses by Analyzing Your Mistakes

Stronger by weakness, wiser men become,
As they draw near to their eternal home.
On the Foregoing Divine Poems, *Edmund Waller*

Bridge, like golf and tennis, is a game of errors. There is no player totally devoid of them, but experts make fewer mistakes than their less accomplished competitors, and therefore win more often and consistently. For this reason, if you want to improve your game, it becomes of paramount importance to recognize the nature of your weaknesses and to work on eliminating, or at least reducing, them.

Are you too aggressive or timid in the bidding? Are you one in competitive auctions but the other in uncontested sequences? Do you lack technical skills in the play of the hand or in defense? Do you pause at trick one, reflect upon the lead and what you see in dummy, and construct a plan? Do you play too quickly and too intuitively and fail to draw the proper inferences? Do you maintain an even tempo so as not to give away your problems? Are you too impulsive, emotional or calm about doing your work? Do you tend to forget which cards were played?

Those are only a few of the long list of questions a serious bridge player with intentions to improve has to ask himself.

Alas, the big problem, the monumental obstacle blocking the road to improvement, is the human ego, and *all* bridge players at *all* levels possess a large dose of it. Humility in recognizing one's weaknesses is very rare, and many a talented player never reaches his full potential, instead lingering complacently on an inferior plateau. He is convinced that there is nothing more to learn because he already knows everything about the game.

A favorite ground for observation and a rich source of

material for my articles is the club game. I like to kibitz because, after all, there one will find more mistakes than brilliancies. The two hands that follow were played by one of our promising young players. He is well versed in card-play technique, he bids with flair, he has no obvious weak points, and is a frequent winner in his circle. This gives him a lot of self-confidence, but has also generated a flaw which will become apparent as we observe these deals.

```
Dlr: West          ♠ 3
Vul: None          ♡ 10 9 8 7 5 4
                   ◇ A 10 9 4
                   ♣ K 3
   ♠ A 5                          ♠ Q 10 9 7 6 2
   ♡ A Q J 6 3                    ♡ 2
   ◇ Q                            ◇ J 3 2
   ♣ Q 8 7 4 2                    ♣ J 6 5
                   ♠ K J 8 4
                   ♡ K
                   ◇ K 8 7 6 5
                   ♣ A 10 9
```

West	North	East	South
West	*North*	*East*	*South*
1 ♡	Pass	Pass	Double
Pass	Pass	1 ♠	Double
2 ♣	Pass	Pass	2 ◇
Pass	3 ◇	Pass	5 ◇
Pass	Pass	Pass	

After the opening lead of the ace of hearts, West cashed the ace of spades and switched to the four of clubs. Without hesitation, declarer played low from the dummy, won with the ace in hand, cashed the king of spades, ruffed a spade in the dummy and led a low heart to his hand for a ruff. This permitted East to get rid of his third club. Belatedly, declarer cashed the

209

king of clubs, but now there was no way to ruff his club loser in the dummy without the loss of a trump trick: one down.

Declarer realized, of course, where he had erred. He should have won trick three with dummy's king of clubs and immediately played a club to the ace, cashed the king of spades and ruffed his last club in the dummy. Now a heart ruff in hand, a spade ruff in the dummy and another heart ruff gives this position:

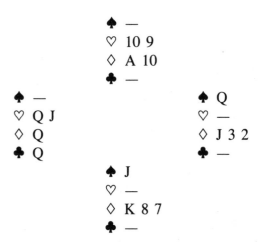

The jack of spades is led and the defense is helpless. If West ruffs with the queen of diamonds, dummy overruffs and the ten is run through East. If West discards, dummy ruffs with the ten of diamonds, the ace is cashed and East's trumps are couped.

Eight boards later, this hand cropped up:

Dlr: West   ♠ 10 2
Vul: E-W   ♡ A 9 8 4 3
               ◊ K 8 5 4
               ♣ 6 3

♠ K Q 4 3		♠ A J 9 6	
♡ Q 6 5		♡ K J 10 7	
◊ A J 2		◊ 3	
♣ K J 2		♣ Q 10 5 4	

               ♠ 8 7 5
               ♡ 2
               ◊ Q 10 9 7 6
               ♣ A 9 8 7

West	*North*	*East*	*South*
1NT	Pass	2♣	2◊ !
2♠	3◊	4♠	5◊ !
Double	Pass	Pass	Pass

West, who obviously did not read my book on trump leads and was influenced by his diamond holding, started with the king of spades. If he had led a trump, an 800-point penalty would not have been difficult to obtain. West continues with two more rounds of trumps the first time he regains the lead, thus restricting declarer to two aces, four trump tricks in hand and one ruff in the dummy.

After the actual spade lead and continuation, East won the second trick with the ace and switched to the four of clubs, which South correctly ducked. West won with the jack and switched to the five of hearts, dummy's ace winning the trick. At this point it looked as though declarer would hold his further losses to two trump tricks and escape with a 500-point penalty and a top. But something went wrong. Declarer ruffed a heart in hand and then erred by playing the queen of diamonds, which West ducked. A spade ruff in the dummy, a heart ruff in hand and the ace of clubs led to the following four-card ending:

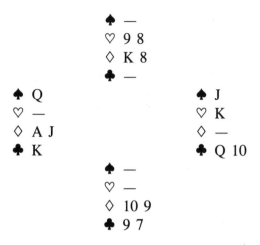

No matter what South led, West had to make two more trump tricks, drawing the outstanding trumps in the process and collecting 800 for a top instead of a bottom.

Had South not made the mistake of playing a trump at trick six, instead cashing the ace of clubs, ruffing a club and a spade in the dummy, and trumping a heart in hand, the four-card ending would have been:

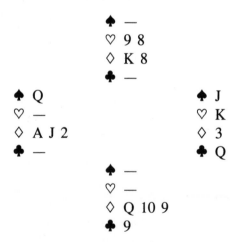

Now declarer ruffs the eight of hearts with the queen of diamonds or, if the lead is in hand, leads the nine of clubs, and the defenders can only take two more tricks.

Analyzing declarer's errors on both hands, we find that he was guilty of:

1. playing too quickly in difficult contracts,
2. lack of proper planning,
3. using his entries in the wrong order, and
4. failure to recognize (in hand two) that a three-trick set would be an excellent score.

This is a good place to end this book, which I hope will have helped you to improve your results. In my early days of competition, I was frequently guilty of making the same types of errors. This was mercilessly pointed out to me by my unforgettable friend and mentor, the late, great Johnny Gerber. It occurred to me that it would be a good idea to keep a little black book, not for my brilliancies but for my bad plays. I was curious whether there was a pattern to the inaccuracies, and whether I was inclined to repeat a certain type of mistake. It helped my game immensely by creating an acute awareness of lurking dangers in some areas, and it spurred my desire to avoid them. Based on experience, I can recommend to you:

My Final Tip for a Top

Be critical of yourself; analyze your mistakes; learn to know your weaknesses; and work out how to correct them.
   Good luck!

Rosenkranz, George
BID YOUR WAY TO THE TOP

An effective standard style with special tools to enable you to reach the correct contract more often. Recommended for: intermediate through expert.

Hard Cover $5.95

Rosenkranz, George
BRIDGE: THE BIDDER'S GAME

Bidding for the 80's; the concepts top experts are using today to increase their slam, game, part score, and competitive accuracy. Included are: an introduction to relays and how they can be incorporated into your present system, trump-asking and control-asking bids, new methods of cue bidding, revisions of popular conventions such as Stayman and Splinter bids, and a complete update of the Romex System, with hundreds of examples. Recommended for: advanced through expert.

Paperback $12.95

Rosenkranz, George
EVERYTHING YOU EVER WANTED TO KNOW ABOUT TRUMP LEADS

A detailed discussion of a subject that confuses even the best players. Chapters include when not to lead trumps, leading trumps to protect high card strength, cutting down ruffing potential, clues from doubles, deceptive trump leads and passive trump leads. Recommended for: intermediate through expert.

Paperback $7.95

Rosenkranz, George and Truscott, Alan
MODERN IDEAS IN BIDDING

Mexico's top player combines with the bridge editor of the NEW YORK TIMES to produce a winner's guide to bidding theory. Constructive bidding, slams, preemptive bidding, competitive problems, overcalls and many other valuable concepts are covered in depth. Increase your accuracy with the proven methods which have won numerous National titles and have been adopted by a diverse group of champions. Recommended for: intermediate through expert.

Paperback $9.95

THE CHAMPIONSHIP BRIDGE SERIES
Volume I
No. 1 Popular Conventions by Randy Baron
No. 2 The Blackwood Convention by E. Blackwood
No. 3 The Stayman Convention by Paul Soloway
No. 4 Jacoby Transfer Bids by Oswald Jacoby
No. 5 Negative Doubles by Alvin Roth
No. 6 Weak Two Bids by Howard Schenken
No. 7 Defense Against Strong Club Opening by K. Wei
No. 8 Killing Their No Trump by Ron Andersen
No. 9 Splinter Bids by Andrew Bernstein
No. 10 Michaels Cue Bid by Michael Passell
No. 11 The Unusual Notrump by Alvin Roth
No. 12 Opening Leads by Robert Ewen
Volume II
No. 13 More Popular Conventions by Randy Baron
No. 14 Major Suit Raises by Oswald Jacoby
No. 15 Swiss Team Tactics by C. and T. Sanders
No. 16 Match Point Tactics by Ron Andersen
No. 17 Overcalls by Mike Lawrence
No. 18 Balancing by Mike Lawrence
No. 19 The Weak Notrump by Judi Radin
No. 20 One Notrump Forcing by Alan Sontag
No. 21 Flannery by William Flannery
No. 22 Drury by Kerri Shuman
No. 23 Doubles by Bobby Goldman
No. 24 Opening Preempts by Robert Hamman
Volume III
No. 25 Popular Systems I by A. Bernstein and R. Baron
No. 26 Popular Systems II by A. Bernstein and R. Baron
No. 27 Lebensohl by Eric Rodwell
No. 28 New Minor Forcing & Fourth Suit Forcing and Artificial by Jeff Meckstroth
No. 29 Minor Suit Raises by Marty Bergen
No. 30 Sacrifices by Bobby Wolff
No. 31 Is It Forcing? by Jim Jacoby
No. 32 2♣ — Strong, Artificial and Forcing by Mary Jane Farell
No. 33 Slam Bidding by Dr. G. Rosenkranz
No. 34 Counting by Ron Andersen
No. 35 Squeeze Play by Robert Hamman
No. 36 Modern Defensive Signals by K. Woolsey

In-depth discussions of the most widely used conventions . . . how to play them, when to use them and how to defend against them. The solution for those costly partnership misunderstandings. Written by some of the world's top experts. 95¢ each

THE CHAMPIONSHIP BRIDGE SERIES
95¢ each
Any 12 for $9.95
Any 24 for $17.90
All 36 for $25.95
(No further discount)

ORDER FORM

Number
Wanted

_____	TOURNAMENT BRIDGE COMPUTER PROGRAM (Apple or IBM)...	x $49.95 =	_____
_____	HOW TO READ OPPONENTS' CARDS, Lawrence	x 7.95 =	_____
_____	FALSECARDS, Lawrence	x 9.95 =	_____
_____	BEGINNING BRIDGE COMPLETE, Penick	x 5.95 =	_____
_____	CLOBBER THEIR ARTIFICIAL CLUB, Baron-Woolsey	x 2.95 =	_____
_____	CARD COMBINATIONS, Lawrence	x 9.95 =	_____
_____	TIPS FOR TOPS, Rosenkranz	x 9.95 =	_____
_____	EVERYTHING YOU EVER WANTED TO KNOW ABOUT TRUMP LEADS, Rosenkranz	x 7.95 =	_____
_____	CARD PLAY FUNDAMENTALS, Blackwood-Hanson	x 5.95 =	_____
_____	COUNTDOWN TO BETTER BRIDGE, Kelsey	x 9.95 =	_____
_____	PLAY IT AGAIN, SAM, Reese-Hoffman	x 7.95 =	_____
_____	BIDDING CHALLENGE, Wolff	x 5.95 =	_____
_____	DO YOU KNOW YOUR PARTNER?, Bernstein-Baron	x 1.95 =	_____
_____	COMPLETE BOOK OF OPENING LEADS, Blackwood	x 12.95 =	_____
_____	HAVE I GOT A STORY FOR YOU!, Eber and Freeman	x 7.95 =	_____
_____	THE FLANNERY TWO DIAMOND CONVENTION, Flannery	x 7.95 =	_____
_____	TABLE TALK, Goodwin	x 5.95 =	_____
_____	THE ART OF LOGICAL BIDDING, Gorski	x 4.95 =	_____
_____	INDIVIDUAL CHAMPIONSHIP BRIDGE SERIES (Please specify)	x .95 =	_____
_____	BRIDGE CONVENTIONS COMPLETE, Kearse (Paperback)	x 17.95 =	_____
_____	BRIDGE CONVENTIONS COMPLETE, Kearse (Hardcover)	x 24.95 =	_____
_____	101 BRIDGE MAXIMS, Kelsey	x 7.95 =	_____
_____	DYNAMIC DEFENSE, Lawrence	x 2.95 =	_____
_____	PARTNERSHIP UNDERSTANDINGS, Lawrence	x 2.95 =	_____
_____	PLAY BRIDGE WITH MIKE LAWRENCE, Lawrence	x 9.95 =	_____
_____	WINNING BRIDGE INTANGIBLES, Lawrence and Hanson	x 2.95 =	_____
_____	TICKETS TO THE DEVIL, Powell	x 5.95 =	_____
_____	PLAY THESE HANDS WITH ME, Reese	x 7.95 =	_____
_____	BRIDGE: THE BIDDER'S GAME, Rosenkranz	x 12.95 =	_____
_____	MODERN IDEAS IN BIDDING, Rosenkranz-Truscott	x 9.95 =	_____
_____	TEST YOUR PLAY AS DECLARER, VOL. 1, Rubens-Lukacs	x 5.95 =	_____
_____	TEST YOUR PLAY AS DECLARER, VOL. 2, Rubens-Lukacs	x 5.95 =	_____
_____	DEVYN PRESS BOOK OF BRIDGE PUZZLES, #1, Sheinwold	x 5.95 =	_____
_____	DEVYN PRESS BOOK OF BRIDGE PUZZLES, # 2, Sheinwold	x 4.95 =	_____
_____	DEVYN PRESS BOOK OF BRIDGE PUZZLES, # 3, Sheinwold	x 4.95 =	_____
_____	STANDARD PLAYS OF CARD COMBINATIONS FOR CONTRACT BRIDGE, Truscott, Gordy and Gordy	x 6.95 =	_____
_____	PARTNERSHIP DEFENSE, Woolsey	x 8.95 =	_____
_____	MATCHPOINTS, Woolsey	x 9.95 =	_____

SPORTS TITLES

_____	OFFICIAL KENTUCKY DERBY QUIZ BOOK, Baron-Von Borries	x 11.95 =	_____
_____	OFFICIAL U. OF KENTUCKY BASKETBALL BOOK, Baron-Rice	x 9.95 =	_____
_____	AMAZING BASKETBALL BOOK, Hill-Baron	x 7.95 =	_____

*QUANTITY DISCOUNT
ON ABOVE ITEMS:
10% over $35, 20% over $75*

SUBTOTAL [_____]

LESS QUANTITY DISCOUNT [_____]

ADD $1.00
SHIPPING
PER ORDER

We accept checks, money orders and VISA or MASTER CARD. For charge card orders, send your card number and expiration date.

TOTAL FOR BOOKS [_____]
SHIPPING ALLOWANCE [_____]
AMOUNT ENCLOSED [_____]

NAME_____

ADDRESS _____

CITY_____ STATE_____ ZIP_____

West Hands

If the stated opposition bidding is insufficient, assume they pass.

1. N-S vul.; IMPs; dealer West.
   - ♠ A K Q 9 4 3
   - ♡ A 9 6 4 3
   - ◊ —
   - ♣ A 10

   (Page 12)

2. E-W vul.; pairs; dealer West. North bids 2♣, showing spades and diamonds; South bids 2♠; North bids 3♠.
   - ♠ A Q
   - ♡ A Q J 4
   - ◊ 8 7
   - ♣ A J 10 5 4

   (Page 20)

3. E-W vul.; pairs; dealer East. South bids 4◊.
   - ♠ K J 9 4
   - ♡ Q 7 5 2
   - ◊ K 2
   - ♣ 7 6 2

   (Page 31)

4. N-S vul.; pairs; dealer East.
   - ♠ A 7 4
   - ♡ K J 9 8
   - ◊ K J 9 8 6
   - ♣ 4

   (Page 33)

5. None vul.; pairs; dealer West.
    ♠ —
    ♡ K Q 9 6 4 2
    ◊ A K 7 5 3
    ♣ A K

(Page 37)

6. None vul.; pairs; dealer West.
South bids 1♠; North bids 3♠.
    ♠ J 2
    ♡ K 7 6
    ◊ A Q 10 7 5
    ♣ Q 4 3

(Page 40)

7. Both vul.; IMPs; dealer East. South
bids 4◊; North bids 5◊.
    ♠ K 10 5 4
    ♡ J 9 8 6 3 2
    ◊ —
    ♣ K 7 2

(Page 47)

8. Both vul.; pairs; dealer East. South
doubles a 1◊ opening; North bids
1♠.
    ♠ Q 10 7 4
    ♡ K Q 3
    ◊ Q J
    ♣ A 9 7 2

(Page 52)

9. None vul.; pairs; dealer West.
   ♠ A 5
   ♡ A Q 8 4
   ◊ Q J 9 3 2
   ♣ 8 6

(Page 65)

10. None vul.; pairs; dealer East.
    ♠ A K 8 5
    ♡ A Q J 9 2
    ◊ 10
    ♣ K 8 2

(Page 66)

11. Both vul.; pairs; dealer East.
    ♠ K
    ♡ A Q 6
    ◊ K J 10 5
    ♣ K 10 6 5 4

(Page 67)

12. None vul.; pairs; dealer West.
    ♠ K Q 10
    ♡ K 7
    ◊ K Q 8
    ♣ A K Q J 5

(Page 68)

13. None vul.; pairs; dealer West.
    ♠ A Q J
    ♡ 9 7
    ◊ K Q 8
    ♣ A K Q J 5

(Page 70)

14. None vul.; pairs; dealer East.
   ♠ 10 6 4 2
   ♡ 8 3
   ◇ K J 8 4
   ♣ Q J 10

(Page 71)

East Hands

If the stated opposition bidding is insufficient, assume they pass.

1. N-S vul.; IMPs; dealer West.
   ♠ 8 6 5
   ♡ K
   ♢ A 10 9 6
   ♣ K 9 8 5 2

   (Page 12)

2. E-W vul.; pairs; dealer West. North bids 2♣, showing spades and diamonds; South bids 2♠; North bids 3♠.
   ♠ 5
   ♡ K 7 6
   ♢ A K 9 6 5
   ♣ K 9 3 2

   (Page 20)

3. E-W vul.; pairs; dealer East. South bids 4♢.
   ♠ A 7 5
   ♡ A 10 6 4 3
   ♢ 3
   ♣ K Q 8 5

   (Page 31)

4. N-S vul.; pairs; dealer East.
   ♠ K 10 8 3
   ♡ A Q 10 5
   ♢ 5
   ♣ A Q 10 2

   (Page 33)

5. None vul.; pairs; dealer West.

♠ A K 3
♡ 10 8 7 5 3
◇ J
♣ Q 7 5 4

(Page 37)

6. None vul.; pairs; dealer West. South bids 1♠; North bids 3♠.

♠ Q 8 3
♡ A Q 10 5
◇ J 6 4
♣ K 5 2

(Page 40)

7. Both vul.; IMPs; dealer East. South bids 4◇; North bids 5◇.

♠ Q J 9 7 2
♡ K Q 5 4
◇ 7
♣ A 5 3

(Page 47)

8. Both vul.; pairs; dealer East. South doubles a 1◇ opening; North bids 1♠.

♠ —
♡ 8 2
◇ A K 10 8 7 2
◇ K Q J 10 4

(Page 52)

9. None vul.; pairs; dealer West.
   - ♠ K Q 10 9 7 2
   - ♡ 3
   - ◊ K 10 8 7 5
   - ♣ A

(Page 65)

10. None vul.; pairs; dealer East.
   - ♠ 6 4
   - ♡ K
   - ◊ A 8 7 6 2
   - ♣ A Q 9 5 3

(Page 66)

11. Both vul.; pairs; dealer East.
   - ♠ A Q 10 7 5
   - ♡ K J 8
   - ◊ 3
   - ♣ Q J 8 7

(Page 67)

12. None vul.; pairs; dealer West.
   - ♠ A J 2
   - ♡ 9 3 2
   - ◊ A J 10 7
   - ♣ 8 7 4

(Page 68)

13. None vul.; pairs; dealer West.
   - ♠ K 10 2
   - ♡ K 3 2
   - ◊ A J 10 7
   - ♣ 8 7 4

(Page 70)

14. None vul.; pairs; dealer East.
   ♠ A K Q 9 5
   ♡ K Q J 10 2
   ◊ 5
   ♣ A K

(Page 71)